*Edited by* LIAM SWORDS

# Funeral
# Homilies

**PAULIST PRESS**
New York ● Mahwah

Published by arrangement with
The Columba Press, Dublin

First published in the United States by
PAULIST PRESS
997 Macarthur Boulevard
Mahwah, N.J. 07430

Library of Congress Catalog Card No: 85-62462

ISBN 0-8091-2784-9

Printed in the Republic of Ireland

# CONTENTS

## 5. Death After a Long Illness

## 6. Death of a Handicapped Person

## 7. Death of the Elderly

# PREFACE

Death is a private affair. A funeral is a public occasion. Grief is borne only by the immediate family and close friends, that little band of bereaved clustered round the remains. The funeral provides the liturgy where, for a brief interval, grief can be contained while the final separation takes place. It employs a language, chiselled out over centuries, to comfort the grief-stricken where ordinary words fail. Ritual, mercifully, accommodates private grief and public sympathy.

The funeral homily attempts to bridge that awesome gap, to make the private public and the public private, to give the bereaved the community's hope in the resurrection and to confront the community with the ultimate reality of individual death. It can be a time of great grace for all. It is always a difficult time for the priest. He runs the risk of intruding insensitively upon a family's grief or of meandering meaninglessly through clichéd formalities.

Funerals, like death, are always unexpected. Priests often have no longer than the night before to prepare a homily. This collection should prove a useful resource for him, permitting him to draw upon a wide pastoral experience, from prison-chaplain to bishop, monk to parish priest. These are not readymade homilies but reflective pieces by theologians, liturgists, scripture scholars, historians, journalists, broadcasters and authors. In the end each priest must give his own homily: each has his own rich ore to mine. They may help him discover it.

*Liam Swords*

# 1

# Death of a Young Person

## *Providence*

*Readings:* Is 25:6-9. Ps 23 *Good Shepherd Psalm.* Mt 5:1-12

God's ways are not our ways. How often we hear that. But it is a true consolation. Sorrow, strife, disaster prompt us to ask what life is all about. Death does too. There is another side – joy, happiness, laughter, celebration. We would not like to think that these would all come to an end. It is as if the pendulum of the human spirit swings between optimism and despair. Faith is our consolation, faith in God's providence. God brings everything to the good. Isaiah puts it in a beautiful way: 'On this mountain he will remove the mourning veil covering all peoples.' Our God is a God of love and mercy, the God of the invisible who sees justice, goodness, and love grow slowly within our hearts. He is patient enough to overlook our faults.

From the cradle to the grave. How short life is. Every time we gather for a funeral, family, friends, parishioners, priest, the thought disturbs. Death sweeps young and old in its path. This death points to our death. Only sometimes, when we ponder on mankind as young on a young planet in a seemingly ageless universe, do we grasp a little notion of eternity. God sees us outside time. To God a thousand years are as one. He sees beyond the trouble and the strife. He sees the seeds of everlasting life, sown by his Son Jesus Christ, fermenting and growing in his new children. God smiles down benevolently on this world.

Death brings sadness. The parting is always sore. At a time of mourning memories flood back. Like the sunshine, it is the virtues and the smiling face we remember. The neighbours understand. They crowd round awkwardly. Sometimes lost for words. Sometimes stumbling over worn phrases. But they are crowding round to support. They want us to lean on them in our grief. The great respectful silence, the murmur of prayer in the church and at the graveside, are simply the love of our brothers and sisters, bolstering our faith even though pain does not lift easily. The family extends beyond the front seats of the Church and the edge of the grave to our brothers and sisters in Christ, extends in prayer to our heavenly

1

Father and to Mary our Mother who stood at the cross when her son was dying. Theirs is true communion with our brother/sister in the family of God.

Our Lord in the Sermon on the Mount, his first sermon, swings the pendulum between life and death, joy and sorrow. This is our consolation. We know that there cannot be an end to all the goodness, concern, compassion, kindness, love of people when they die. These follow them all the days of their life and into the Lord's own house.

> Happy are those who know they are spiritually poor;
> The kingdom of heaven belongs to them.
> Happy are those who mourn;
> God will comfort them.

These are the promises – the kingdom of heaven, comfort, full satisfaction, mercy, the vision of God, great reward for those who are pure of heart, who live spiritually, humbly, mercifully, in accordance with God's will. To the world it is a contradiction that Christ equates persecution and mourning with happiness. God's ways are not our ways.

But this is the good news of Christ who by dying destroyed our death and by rising restored our life. Real optimism. Christ continually emphasises that sorrow will be turned into joy.

We have to live in time, imprisoned by our limitations. When someone near to us dies, we have to pick up the pieces and start again. But nothing is happening without a purpose, without God turning it to the good. The cup of cold water given in the name of God has its reward. God is personal and we know him from Christ as a Father:

> Look at the birds flying around: they do not sow seeds, gather a harvest and put it in barns; yet your Father in heaven takes care of them. Aren't you worth much more than birds? Can any of you live a bit longer by worrying about it?

We must not grieve too much. We are caught up in God's created time and must continue our work. Each day its duty. Deep down is faith and hope. Sorrow is turned into joy. We do not always understand. God's ways are not our ways. But we believe he is our providence and he will bring us safely home, even if we walk through the valley of darkness. Like Jesus we abandon ourselves into his hands. Then we are blessed with salvation and eternal glory.

*Raymond Murray*

2

# Red Rose

*Readings:* Lam 3:22-26. Rom 14:7-9. Mk 10:13-16

It is so hard to believe that Rose is no longer with us. She was very much a part of our lives. We took her for granted. Now all we have are memories. All these little things she used, all those photographs, those souvenirs and pictures, only give a half-image of a loved one. The pain and the real image are carried in the heart.

As we all gather here for the funeral, we must remind ourselves that death is a very private thing. It is a family and personal occasion. No matter how hard we try, we cannot share our sorrow with strangers. One red rose on a grave speaks more than a shop full of wreaths. Death, like love, is a very intimate thing, too precious even to speak about.

However, if death is a private occasion, a funeral is a public occasion. A funeral is our way of saying thanks to someone for having shared her life with us, her parents and friends. A funeral is an act of love – the last act of love. It is the time when a family share its love for its lost one. And it is fitting that all this happens in the context of the Mass, for the Mass is the great act of thanksgiving, of thanking God for having sent his Son and redeemed the world. We likewise thank God for having sent us Rose who was with us for so very short a time, but who gave us such joy and happiness during that short time.

A funeral is also a giving, a giving up of one's beloved, a giving back to God. It is a sacrifice. It is only in the context of our Lord's passion and death that we can penetrate the mystery of suffering, and understand the real meaning of the word sacrifice. We are called on to make so many sacrifices during our lifetime, but the loss of a dear child is the supreme sacrifice. Only love can triumph over such a loss, for St Paul assures us that 'love does not come to an end' (1 Cor 13:8). The liturgy of death is an Easter liturgy: 'Dying, Christ destroyed our death, and rising, he restored our life.' As indeed he will one day restore to life our beloved Rose.

A funeral tells us in a vivid way how passing is the world we live in, how short a time we all have here on earth. Young people are so full of life, of exuberance, of vitality, always running here and there. Rose has not stopped running, only this time she has run into the arms of God. I somehow feel that the gates of heaven are left open on such an occasion, so that she did not have to knock on the door.

*Mark Tierney OSB*

# Bright Promise

Reading: 2 P 3:3-10

At eighteen, the world was at his feet. Life was all before him and he reached out and grabbed it with both hands. Watching him play football – a mere six months ago – he seemed to be everywhere on the pitch, pushing himself to the limit and beyond, urging his team mates to ever greater efforts. He was the same in the classroom.

There was an open-minded, alert eagerness about him that challenged his teacher and his classmates alike. His name cropped up frequently in the staff-room. 'A promising student' was the unanimous opinion. 'The lad has a bright future.' But his days were brutally numbered. Cancer was already eating its way into a young man's springtime. Nobody dreamt that the classmates who carried him shoulder high from the pitch after the last match, would carry him shoulder high so soon again – this time to the cemetery.

A young life, full of promise, nipped in the bud. A father and mother who birthed him, nursed him, reared him and lavished on him ungrudgingly the best years of their lives – to have him snatched away. A school, a community that nurtured his talents and mapped out his future – robbed of their prize. All now huddled in grief round the remains of a dream. It seems so senseless and so cruel. As if God was a spoilt child tiring quickly of his latest toy.

Creatures are not the Creator's puppets, dancing while he cares to pull the strings. Their life is not measured by hours or days or years, the duration of the Creator's whimsy. A life-span is just as complete at eighteen as at eighty. 'There is one thing, my friends, you must never forget,' Peter said, 'that with the Lord a day can mean a thousand years and a thousand years is like a day' (2 P 3:8). A life once lived achieves its full potential. The purpose of life is living. 'Many a flower is born to blush unseen and waste its sweetness on the desert air.'

Each life, like each flower is a unique creation. It mirrors its creator, no matter how brief its existence. Flowers have only to blossom. They are often most radiant just before they fade.

What about all the promise, never to be realised? Religion has always tried to probe the beyond for an answer. For pre-Christian celts, paradise was *tír na nóg*, the land of eternal youth. The Greeks came up with the expression, 'those whom the gods love die young'. The list of those who did is impressive – from John the Baptist to Mozart and John F. Kennedy. God himself took his only Son Jesus in his early thirties. All cut down in the prime of life. Some had already

4

achieved great things. All showed enormous promise.

Today's promises never find fulfilment in this world's tomorrow. Those who survive to middle age and beyond are incontestable proof of that. Life is strewn with broken promises. Golden haired youths seldom grow to greatness. Those who die in their spring may well be spared a winter of discontent. 'We want you to be quite certain, brothers, about those who have died,' Paul told the Thessalonians, 'to make sure that you do not grieve about them, like the other people who have no hope. We believe that Jesus died and rose again and that it will be the same for those who have died in Jesus. God will bring them with him' (1 Thess 4: 13,14). To the Promised Land, the land of promise, where the saints go marching in. The Preface says it all: 'The sadness of death gives way to the bright promise of immortality.'

*Liam Swords*

# A Rosy Future

*Reading:* Jn 20:11-18

To be a Christian is to be a pilgrim. To be a pilgrim is to go along the way of faith, hope and love. The goal is certain, eternal life in Christ Jesus our Lord. But the way is very uncertain. The way comes to an end for some in childhood, for others in ripe old age.

For the deceased it has tragically come to an end in her early twenties, when she has everything going for her, in the prime of life, full of vitality, possessing grace, charm and beauty, having a sense of fun, scores of friends, a job, a rosy future, a good home, loving parents, a loving brother. Today our hearts are broken; our spirits are crushed with the suddeness of it all. It's only human that we should shed tears and give vent to our grief. Tears can have a healing effect. So can the presence, the support and the sensitivity of so many friends and relatives present here this morning. So can the familiar rite of the Mass, the word proclaimed, the bread broken and shared. The Mass can speak to us with extraordinary power on an occasion like this.

All of these will sustain us in the bleak days ahead. There is a tendency to want to cling on to the one who has left us, telling the same story again and again, pointing to the pictures on the wall, the room they occupied, to the time of day they went out or came in. But the secret of mourning is not to want to cling on but to let go, to allow them to die a little more to us each day so that we can possess them and relate to them in a new way. That is where faith comes to the rescue. That is how the Gospel story becomes our story. We recall the admonition of Christ to Mary Magdalen: 'Do not cling to me.'

The long period of mourning was necessary for the disciples before they were able to receive the consolation of the Spirit, but with the Spirit they possess the one whose death had left them desolate. They begin to possess him and to relate to him in a new way. We pray that our mourning may not make us less human but more Christian. Our letting go can bring us to deep peace in the Holy Spirit, a peace we never dreamt possible, a peace which surpasses all understanding.

*Eltin Griffin OCarm*

# Fullness of Life

*Readings:* Lam 3:17-26. Jn 12:23-28. Mk 15:33-39

The shock of this tragedy has stunned the whole parish. For those of us who knew Mary, this occasion in the church has an air of unreality about it. We cannot believe what has happened. For her parents and family the event is a nightmare from which they would hope to awaken. The suddenness of Mary's passing leaves us stunned by grief.

We know that, however hard we try, none of us can really enter into the desolate world of her father and mother and share their pain of loss. Their sorrow is something that only they themselves can know. This kind of bereavement is stark, private, and exclusive. In this sense, we are all outsiders at this moment of their mourning. God and his love may well have become emotionally eclipsed as we are gripped in a heartbreak that is bleakest and most vacant of all. Although we stand alone before the tragic mystery of death, nevertheless Mary's natural family are here as members of a larger family: their family of faith, the local Christian community. We are all bound to each other by the special form of friendship that is the friendship of faith.

This whole community believes that Jesus Christ has gone through death before us and has conquered the evil of death so that we might have the strength to face it in our own lives. Mary of Nazareth had an only child who suffered a violent death before her eyes. She too has experienced the unspeakable sorrow of sudden bereavement. But we know that Jesus went through his violent death that we might have life. The events of his death and resurrection are a mystery that we enter into through faith, and only through faith. The Christian community here offers this faith by their prayerful presence. As we celebrate this sacrifice of the Mass, we lean on the love of one another. Hard pressed as our faith may be, the solidarity of our friendship in faith will hold us together in hope, in hope of everlasting life. We are confident that Mary is enjoying a fullness of life with God that is beyond our human comprehension: a fulfilment that for her will last forever.

*Tom Stack*

# Nearer than the Door

*Readings:* Jn 19:25-42. Rom 4:13-18

St Paul tells his newly converted Christian people that they are not 'to grieve about those who have died, like the other people who have no hope.' Does this mean that Christians are not supposed to grieve at the death of a family member or close friend? Is the Christian not to feel shock, the sense of loss, the deep pain which a sudden death brings in its wake? Yes, he is surely! For the Christian, as for the unbeliever, there is no such thing as death without tears. Our Lord shared the grief of his friends Mary and Martha when he cried openly at the tomb of Lazarus. Jesus was truly God and truly man, and he was truly moved to the depths of his being at the sight of his friends in their sorrow.

But the crucial difference between the Christian and the pagan in the face of death is not in the depth of grief which each will feel at the time, but in the firm belief of the Christian that all is not lost, that the parting is not permanent.

This reaction to the event can be illustrated by the words of an Irish country woman who was poor and without much formal education, but rich in Christian faith. Peig Sayers lived her life on the rocks of the Blasket Islands; her life was always a struggle. She knew the anxious nights when her husband and his friends were out in fishing boats. She feared the knock on the door which would bring bad news. The bad news came when her twenty-year old son fell to his death over a cliff as he pulled roots for firewood. Like the parents present today, she was heartbroken. But she was turning instinctively to her true friends for the meaning of this tragedy and for the strength to sustain her in her grief. Here is what she said about her sorrow:

> We wouldn't have minded the hardship of life, however, but for the fact that death was gathering his strength behind it. But that rascal too has to get what's due to him.
>
> I remember well when I was trying to work, while at the same time the heart in my breast was broken by sorrow, that I'd turn my thoughts on Mary and on the Lord, and on the life of hardship they endured. I knew that it was my duty to imitate them and to bear my cross in patience. Often I'd take my little canvas sheet and face for the hill for a small amount of turf and on the road home the weight on my heart would have lifted. God's Son and his glorious Mother are true friends!

For Peig Sayers and her generation, who lived close to God and to nature, it was second nature to them to turn to Jesus and Mary when trouble came to their door. *Is giorra cabhar Dé ná an doras* was their proverb. (God's help is nearer than the door.)

At this time you, dear friends, who are shocked and full of grief, may experience regrets. You may find yourselves agonising over the might-have-beens. You may experience feelings of anger and be tempted to blame yourselves or to blame others. Please, be careful about such feelings. They are part of the grieving process. They are normal at this time. But they can be dangerous if you allow them to linger too long. Confide them to our Lord and to his Mother. After that, tell them only to very close friends who will help you come to terms with your grief. Then you will grieve like a Christian. You overcome your hurt and do not pass it on to others.

Let me leave you with Our Lord's assurance to his disciples whom he knew would mourn his going from them: 'You will have sorrow, but your sorrow will be turned into joy!'

*Dermot Clifford*

# Eternal Youth

*Reading:* Mt 22:23-33

A death, especially a sudden one, very often reveals the real values of the people associated with it. Christians who have worked on their faith and have struggled to understand God's ways with us will be well able to cope with the full meaning of death for a Christian. For such people the liturgical and scriptural texts will seem a natural statement of what they think always about death. The death of a young person seems particularly repugnant to the secular mentality because it is felt that there is now no opportunity to live life at all. It is more of a riddle than the death of an elderly person whose time has come anyway. We do not often question why death should come to any human being, or even why people grow old at all, so hypnotised are we by the ideal of youthfulness as the full way of being human.

Christian faith does not pretend that the death of any human being is other than a mystery, and one that causes deep pain and loss. It recognises that the death of a younger person is particularly absurd because the promise of a human being with his/her life yet to live is frustrated. We Christians believe that God calls us to live a life that is fully human, to realise the gifts and talents that he himself has given us, to make a worthwhile contribution to our fellowmen and women, to love and be loved. The cutting off of such possibilities challenges us very profoundly. If God is the lover and supreme affirmer of human beings and of their projects and dreams, then he cannot be indifferent to the death of a young person who has not had the chance to realise his human potential.

But God is the God of the living and not of the dead. He is the God of Abraham, Isaac, and Jacob. He is the God of people who live. God showed the immensity of his love for human beings and for their hopes and aspirations when he put the fullness of his life-giving power at their service, when he defeated the power of evil, sin and death and raised Jesus to the fullness of life, a life that is so much life that death has no more power over it. Jesus was not simply raised from the dead to be restored to the same kind of life as he had before the cross. He was utterly transformed so that his humanity could finally realise the fullness of its potential in the presence of God and on behalf of the human race to which he is always present. All those who share his death and resurrection will share in this transformation too. They too will enter into eternal youth and live with and for God. This is the true fulfilment of human beings. *Michael Mulvihill CSSp*

10

# Letting Go

*Reading:* Jn 11:17-27

'If you had been here my brother would not have died.' The Lord was here and yet the deceased died. Today the Lord wants us to weep, to believe, to let go and to give thanks.

The Lord bids us to weep. He himself wept at the grave of Lazarus. So if we want to weep, let us weep; if we want to mourn and lament, by all means let us show our grief because grief is healing and strengthening.

The Lord bids us to believe. The Lord wants us to believe those majestic words of his in the Gospel which has just been proclaimed to us: 'I am the Resurrection and the Life. If anyone believes in me, even though he be dead, he will live and whoever lives and believes in me will never die.' We believe, on the strength of those words, that the deceased has gone into the eternal day, that he has entered into a more total union with the risen Lord of all creation, with all humanity and with the inhabitants of the eternal city.

The Lord bids us to let go. Letting go is very hard. We never want to let go of those who are dear to us. And parents are always letting go from the first day the child goes to school until he leaves home, until he leaves for his eternal home if he is called home before them. The apostles did not want to let go of Christ. But Christ told them if he did not go from them he could not send the Spirit. Mary Magdalen wanted to cling to the risen Jesus. We have to let go of N. but tomorrow and in the years to come, we shall possess him in a new way: we shall possess him in the Spirit.

The Lord bids us to give thanks. As we go from the Liturgy of the Word into the Liturgy of the Eucharist, we unite our thanksgiving with the great thanksgiving of Christ in the Mass. We give thanks for the youth who brought such joy into our lives.

It takes the lived Christian experience to convey the idea of letting go and it takes the poet to put the experience in a nutshell:

I have had worse partings, but none so gnaws at my mind still.
Perhaps it is roughly saying that God alone could perfectly show –
How selfhood begins with a walking away,
And love is proved in the letting go.

(C. Day Lewis: *Walking Away)*

*Eltin Griffin OCarm*

11

# A Gift for Ever

*Reading:* Jn 11:1-4

Whenever someone we love dies we too die a little. We know that we can never be exactly the same again. An area of life – a familiar voice, a footstep, a shared memory – has suddenly disappeared, and cannot ever be recreated. It is a heart-rending experience because the one we loved, and still love, has a place in our hearts and we can no longer find a place in his. A great violence has been done to us because we have lost a place where we loved to rest. So mixed with our sadness there may well be an anger that the balance of our lives has been so roughly upset.

In our different ways we came to know and love this man. He played a part in our lives and helped to make us what we now are. That is the power of love. Our love for him and his love for us has, even if only a little, changed us all.

He was a gift for us, as we were gifts for him. Every good and perfect gift is from above, and a person is a gift which above all others is from God. It is surely true – and we know this instinctively as well as from our own experience – that every true gift has been given for ever. There is no going back on a gift which has been freely made. This person and our love for each other are gifts from God, and we can be quite sure in our heart of hearts as well as in our minds that he will never deprive us of these precious gifts.

His greatest gift to us was his Son, who was given to all people for all time. He died, harshly and surrounded by fear and anger, and then, having passed through death's doorway, he was brought by his Father into a new life of glory. So we proclaim at Mass: 'Dying you destroyed our death, rising you restored our life, Lord Jesus come in glory!' He died to show his friends how they could find their way to their true home.

This man was one of Jesus' friends and he is now being ushered along the way to his place with God. In his lifetime he was a gift to us in so many ways. We have shared in his faith. We have been lifted up by his enthusiasm, cheered by his smile, warmed by his friendship. We are glad in our knowledge that because we were friends we brought each other happiness, for in friendship there is always both giving and receiving.

Now God's gift is returning to him, and the friend whose death we mourn is at home, at rest, at peace. We pray for him in great confidence because he was *God's* friend as well as ours, and friends cannot be kept apart from each other for long. We pray for everyone who has been saddened by his death, that in the desert of their sorrow a deeper love and hope may flower. In our own sadness, though, let us thank God for his gift to us, and pray that, strange though it may be, our loss can become a source for us of a deeper, richer faith. The gift that our friend will yet become for us has not yet been revealed. His life has just begun; our friendship has been renewed. Thanks be to God!

*+David Konstant*

# What are You Talking About?

*Reading:* Lk 24:13-35

St Luke's Gospel tells us of two men whose lives have lost all meaning. The bottom has dropped out of their lives. Jesus meant so much for them. Not just as individuals, but for their families, for their people. They had pinned all their hopes, all their dreams, on Jesus. And now he was dead.

Jesus, they had left in Jerusalem and they walked to somewhere they knew. Back to somewhere familiar. Leaving behind their hopes and their dreams.

And as they walked and they talked Jesus joined them on their journey. They didn't recognise him. He simply joined in their conversation and they did not know who he was. As he walked and talked with them, shared his thoughts with them, he helped them see things in a different light. In fact he made their hearts 'burn within them' as they said.

They came to where they were planning to spend the night and they pressed Jesus to stay with them. They went into the inn and as St Luke says 'they broke bread'. They shared the Eucharist. As they shared they recognised that Jesus had been with them and was with them then. They saw too that Jesus had not left them, but rather was at the heart of all they cared about, all they longed for, all they prayed for. Jesus was there.

The story of those two men going to Emmaus is our story too. We are here at Mass giving thanks for the life of Bernard. Someone who was so important to our lives. Someone on whose life we had pinned so much. Centred our lives on so much. And now he is dead.

So many hopes, so many plans are no more. We can talk all about the things where he was so important. Even as I am talking now I cannot help but see his smiling face, because that was how he always was. Ready to brighten up even the brief moments one had with him. His ready wit. Yet his gentle sensitivity. His real charm. As with you, I am sure you can hear him laugh, see his gestures even now. It is so hard to believe that we will not see him again. Yet, as we walk and talk, sit and think, as the disciples on their walk to Emmaus, what we are asked to know is that Bernard is with us. He is very close, praying for us, loving us, caring for us, cheering us up, in a way much deeper than he has ever done before.

The time when we really become aware of this is when we do what the disciples did on their journey. As they stopped and broke bread and shared the Eucharist – that is what we are doing now. In this very special way we know that the living Lord, the Christ, is with us. And we know that in him we are all together sharing his love and his life. When we gather round the altar we bring bread, we bring wine, we bring what we can touch, what we can feel. What nourishes our bodies and cheers our lives. We do what Jesus told us to do. In doing that we know we are in touch with that which we cannot see or feel. We remember, not just a test of memory, but a living presence – the living Lord. And in him we share, we are one in love and in unity, with a deep peace with those we love, with those we care for. The Lord is risen, he is with us. His promise is ours.

*J. Harry Stratton*

# Why Life, If Death?

*Reading:* Mk 10:16

'Since men have not succeeded in curing death, they have decided not to think about it at all,' remarks Pascal ironically. How false this is when a young life, full of youthful enthusiasm, is snatched from this world. It is inexplicable in human terms. Why is this happening to us? is the first question that springs from the broken hearts of the parents. 'Why life, if death? Why death, if life?' asks the great poet Dante. We are joined together today seeking the first stumbling answers to the 'Why?' of this death. And they will be partial, stumbling answers. Even if we had a perfectly neat solution, the pain in our hearts is too raw to be healed by the balm of words alone.

Your suffering is deep. The truest thing that can be said about suffering is that it is not a problem so much as a mystery. A problem is something you can solve and therefore get rid of. A mystery, one can only become aware of, accept and live. 'Blessed are those who mourn, for they shall be comforted.' So Christ in the second beatitude lifts up the grieving and places them among the poor in spirit, the peacemakers, the merciful, the pure in heart. Jesus promises that they will be comforted. He is concerned with those who grieve. One of his last acts was to entrust his own grieving mother to the care of St John.

Jesus reserved one of the marks of special affection for children. 'He put his arms around them, laid his hands on them and gave them his blessing' (Mk 10:16). Our hope tells us that he is doing that right now with this child. Our hope also assures us that 'we shall all be reunited where tears will be wiped away'. Family and friends will be one again in God's Kingdom. The death of a young person is so tragic. They have everything to live for. And yet their very innocence and beauty is an assurance of their eternal happiness.

A final point, which won't eliminate your suffering but may make it more tolerable, is the fact that Jesus, a young man of thirty-three, went through the same barrier to suffering. His limbs were bruised, his members gashed. St Paul reassures us: 'Christ among you, your hope of glory' (Col 1:27), and St Luke the physician explains: 'Was it not ordained that Christ should suffer and so enter into his glory?' (Lk 24: 25). One of the prophets, Isaiah, foretells of Jesus as 'a man of sorrows and familiar with suffering'. He knows what you are suffering because it was part of his human experience also.

So now we look, not at what might have been, but rather at what is to come. The hope of eternal glory is the comfort of our faith that makes this a day of deep sadness, but behind the sadness the sum of confident hope eases the pain.

*Martin Tierney*

---

*Suggested Alternative Scripture Readings:*

Judges 11:29-40.
2 Samuel 1:23-26.
2 Samuel 19:1-5.

Job 1:18-21.
Psalms 8:1-9. 27:1, 2-10, 13-14. 39:3-9, 12-13. 57:1-3, 7-11. 84:1-9. 86:1-8, 12-13, 15-17. 88:1-5, 10, 13, 14. 131:1-3. 144:1-3.
Ecclesiasticus 17:1-7, 12-13.
Isaiah 25:6-9.
Lamentations 3:17-26.
Joel 1:1-3, 8, 12.

Romans 6:3-4, 8-9. 14:7-9.
1 Corinthians 15:20-23.
Ephesians 1:3-5.
1 Thessalonians 4:13-18.
1 John 3:1-2.
Revelation 7:9-10, 15-17. 21:1, 3-5.

Matthew 5:1-12. 11:25-30. 18:1-4, 10.
Luke 7:11-17. 18:15-17.
John 6:37-40. 6:51-58. 11:32-38, 40 (*child*). 11:32-45. 12:23-38. 14:1-6.

# 2
## Death of a Parent

### We Look for the Resurrection of the Dead

*Readings:* Is 25:6-9. 1 Cor 15:10-12. Jn 17:16-24

Every Sunday at Mass we profess our faith in the resurrection, not only of Jesus of Nazareth, but of every man, woman, and child, from the beginning to the end of human history. It may well be that when we recite the words of the Creed, 'we look for the resurrection of the dead', we give them little more than passing attention. Then comes the day when they take on a deep personal meaning for us, because we are laying to rest someone we love. We look for the resurrection of the dead now because life without that expectation would lack meaning and completeness. At moments like these we are forced to draw seriously on our faith and to explore its meaning with our hearts as well as with our minds.

At moments like these the Holy Spirit of God draws especially close to us because our defences are down and because we now not merely profess, but really experience, our need of him as comforter. It is one of the graces that those we have loved in life bequeath to us when they go before us on the road to God. The Holy Spirit, whom the liturgy speaks of as the 'first gift' of Jesus to those who believe, comes to us as 'the best of comforters'. The comfort he offers us is not a superficial thing removing from us the sorrow and sense of loss we feel. Belief in the resurrection does not relieve us of our grief. Nor should we expect it to come automatically. The affirmation of faith which we are asked to make is too profound and important to be easy.

To all appearances death is a very final thing, and we should not feel that our faith asks us to think otherwise. Faith in the resurrection does not remove our tears; it allows them to glisten faintly in the light that lies beyond, the light in which God himself lives. It is that light which God himself lives. It is that light which helps to explain and give meaning to the sense of incompleteness, the heart-hunger, the instinct within us all that we were made for more than even the loveliest and worthiest of earthly experiences.

Life is a series of adventures, concluding with the greatest adventure of all, when we have done everything that can be done and now must give ourselves over into the hands of the God who made us, and who, through Jesus, has taught us to think of him and approach him as Abba, Father. He has given us a strange, beautiful, and frightening world to live in. As Christians we believe that he shares our life in this bewildering world by sending his Son to be one of us. Jesus spoke, probably often, about the need for the seed to fall into the ground if there was to be a harvest. That is a difficult teaching; but it responds exactly to our experience of life with its blend of light and shade, joy and sorrow, which can be so hard to understand and accept. Instinctively, we would like it otherwise: light without shade. But that is the condition of eternity, and here below we have no way of knowing what such an existence might be like.

God's own Son, at his Father's bequest, took upon himself the dark adventure of death. On the third day his Father raised him from the dead. The Christian Church, from the very first moment of its existence, has believed and preached that what had happened to him would happen to us, for he was the first-fruit of the whole harvest of which we are part. We shall be raised to new life, because he took on himself the experience and the pain of death. That is why, although we mourn the departure of those we love, we do so in the knowledge that we are also celebrating their homecoming.

In the words of a great Indian poet and mystic, 'Death is not extinguishing the light, but putting out the lamp because the dawn has come.'

*Gabriel Daly OSA*

19

# Simple Things

*Reading:* Mt 25:31-46

It happens sometime that what is plainly to be seen is what we fail to see. The simple goodness of ordinary people makes no headlines. It is not news. And thank God for that. It would be a sad day for all of us if goodness were so rare as to be newsworthy. It is only the things that are unusual that arouse our curiosity. Notice how surprised those people were to whom our Lord said: 'I was hungry and you gave me food; I was thirsty and you gave me drink. . .' They could not remember ever having done this. And then our Lord said: 'I tell you solemnly, insofar as you did this to one of the least of these brothers of mine, you did it to me.'

Today we are bringing to burial someone who has done these very things. But we hardly noticed. These things were not newsworthy. They were the realities of their daily living. For, after all, everyone of us came naked from our mother's womb. And we were clothed. And it was our parents who clothed us. We came home hungry and thirsty. And our parents were there to give us food and drink. We were sick and our parents nursed us. And if it should ever be our misfortune to go to prison, though friends might forsake us, we may be sure that our parents would visit us. Every single one of us came into this world as a stranger. And we were welcomed into a happy family home. Those of you who are in mourning today will no doubt be remembering these things.

It is the marvel of our Christian faith that these simple realities of daily living become the seed from which eternal life flowers. It is our faith that life is changed, not taken away. We believe in the resurrection of the dead and the life of the world to come. We thank God for the life which has reached its earthly fulfilment. We thank God for all that we have received. And we pray that our Lord may now speak these words: 'Come, you whom my Father has blessed, take for your heritage the kingdom prepared for you since the foundation of the world.'

*Henry Peel OP*

# The Sadness of Death

*Readings:* 1 Thess 4:13-18. Jn 11:17-27

Today we all feel the sadness of death. We have come to share the sorrow of the family. We have come because we wish to express our sympathy with them and our support for them in their grief and loss. We may find it hard to express that sympathy in words because we feel it so deeply, but we express it at least by our presence here. In coming here we are doing as Jesus did when he went to Bethany and was deeply moved, and even wept, at the grave of his friend, Lazarus. It is right that we, his followers, should share in the sadness of this death.

It is a good and Christian thing to 'weep with those who weep' (Rom 12:15), but St Paul tells us that we should 'not grieve as others do who have no hope' (1 Thess 4). That does not mean that our hope can give us an escape from the sadness of death, but we believe that, behind the sorrow and pain we feel, lies the reality that the deceased is in the hands of God who is infinite mercy and love. He/she has arrived at the destiny for which we all live and hope. So we do grieve, but as people who have hope. Faced with the fact of death, we nevertheless know that if anyone has believed in Christ, 'though he die, yet shall he live' (Jn 11). Our sadness has an underlying current of peace. We have a life which is already free from death. Not only does death not destroy the life we share with Christ, death completes and fulfils it. 'The sadness of death gives way to the bright promise of immortality.' For the Lord's faithful people, 'life is changed, not ended' (Preface of Christian Death 1). Those who have died in Christ have entered a life which is fuller and more glorious than we have ever experienced.

We who are left behind feel the emptiness of their going from us, but for them there is no more sadness. We pray today for the deceased that he/she may be remembered among those who have been raised by God to the fullness of life.

If we live in the light of that hope, the sadness of parting will be followed, at the end of our own lives, by a reunion in which God will wipe away every tear from our eyes (Apoc 21: 4). We who are alive, who are left, will be caught up together with those who have died to meet the Lord. Together 'we shall always be with the Lord. Comfort one another with these words' (1 Thess 4:18).

*+Donal Murray*

# The Will of the Father

*Reading:* Mk 14:36

At such a tragic moment as this words are woefully inadequate. Yet it is important for us to try to articulate the hope that is within us, that hope which sees even Good Friday as the gate to the glory of Easter Sunday. On such occasions we come to church to celebrate, to let Jesus speak to us, to cast some light on the great mystery of suffering and death which envelopes all our lives. If our religion does not really speak to us at such teachable moments it is merely a superficial appendage to our lives.

Although we use the Christian words and gestures yet deep down our thoughts and feelings can so easily be a contradiction. What do we really mean when we pray at such a vital, even tragic moment: 'Thy will be done', words we recall which Jesus himself prayed in Gethsemane:

Abba father, you have the power to do all things.
Take this cup away from me. Not as I will but let it be as you will.

As commentators have pointed out, the meaning of these words depends on the kind of God to whom we speak and on the attitude and feeling we put into the words which we use. By using the unparalleled word *Abba* or *Daddy* for the almighty God, Jesus showed us that even in the darkest and most dreadful hour of our lives we should approach our God with the same attitude as a little child to the parent whom he loves and trusts.

The phrase 'thy will be done' ('by me') was intended to be a battle cry and so easily it becomes a wailing cry or words of weary resignation. For God's will is health not disease, giving not grabbing, love not hate, joy not misery, a positive everlasting life, not a negative depressing death. Jesus invites us to purify our hearts of all bitter resentment, to believe that we are not the playthings of a capricious God, of blind chance and fate. The poet Rainer Maria Rilke expressed this so beautifully:

The leaves are falling, falling down the air,
as though the gardens of the heavens withered,
falling all with gestures of despair;
and in the night the heavy earth is falling
past all the stars, down, down to nothingness.
We are all falling, down to nothingness,

22

Yet there is one who holds the falling
Gently in his hands, with endless gentleness.

Jesus did not just teach us about God. He lived God for us. In Gethsemane Jesus does not explain the mystery of suffering nor does he treat suffering with the indifference of a stoic. But he gives us the example of how to love, how to accept the will of the Father even though it is a mystery. He invites us to have confidence that his will is love and our peace.

*Sean P Kealy CSSp*

# Love Stronger than Death

*Reading:* 1 Cor 12:31–13:8

The death of any Christian concerns each member of the Christian community. That is why the death and burial of any member gives rise to special community activity. The Eucharist is the natural highpoint of all the events that rightly surround the death of a Christian. The Eucharist is a community action. It is both the fullest sign and most effective cause of brotherly solidarity and concern for one another. It is the sacramental expression of the death of the Lord until he comes. It is the presence among us of the Lord's own self-giving that all of us might have life. It is the central and primary means by which God forms and moulds us into a community that cares and shares. It is the experience from which we learn the unique dignity of every person and our solidarity with him/her.

Christians value the family very highly as the intimate community of life and love that is the home of vulnerable persons. The family is the environment of love and care where father and mother relate to one another in love and creative power. It is the community where human persons are introduced into this world with all its hopes and possibilities.

If the couple have had a close relationship with the Lord, if their marriage has been in faith, then the sense of communion will continue beyone the grave, and though the pain of separation will certainly be there, so also will the sense that faith gives of a love stronger than death.

We are all called to put love of God first in our lives and to regulate our other loves in accordance with that greatest of all loves. When the loved partner of a marriage dies the love of God, already experienced and nourished in prayer will be a powerful help for the partner who has to cope with pain, sense of loss, disorientation, the enormous difficulties of readjustment to another way of life, and not least trying, now singlehandedly, to look after the children of the marriage.

If the parent of a young family dies, now is the time for the Christian community which lives by the Eucharist, to find its true identity in it, to become more effectively the sign of God's love and care of his people. Let the church be experienced as church: the mystery of the presence of the living God with and for his people.

*Michael Mulvihill CSSp*

# V-Sign

*Reading:* Jn 14:1

> Do not let your hearts be troubled.
> Trust in God still, and trust in me.
> There are many rooms in my Father's house;
> if there were not, I should have told you.
> I am going now to prepare a place for you.

John would have understood those words of Jesus, for all his own life was spent in preparing places for others. As a young man, he set about making a home for his future wife, Mary; in the years to follow he set aside many of his own personal interests to make a home for his children, and by his example he led the whole family to that home where he is now gone. Come to think of it, this is what we are all about – making room for others on this earth and helping, with Jesus, to prepare a place for ourselves and all dear to us in heaven.

John knew the secret of living well in both worlds – knowing that in truth they were not two separate worlds. He had come to see the glory of God in all his creation. He had made his own the words of the Offertory: 'Blessed are you Lord, God of all creation. . .' It was through the goodness of God he accepted the things of this world and put his own human hands to their making. His work, like his talents, were all gift and he put them to use building up the kingdom of God on this earth. Without spelling it out in religious language, John so acted that the kingdom of God was built up day by day in his work, in his play and in all his many-splendoured relationships. For this man, soul and body, spirit and flesh, prayer and life – these were not separate spheres of existence.

They mingled and informed each other in what might be termed a divine humanity. John was in truth a whole person, who never opted out of life, yet whose eyes were ever on the eternal hills.

The thin veil between heaven and earth was made for distinction, but not for division – a lesson we might all take to heart this day. This is the core of Christianity: the kingdom of God is very near; it is already among you; in the very heart of you. It seeps into the stuff of daily living, so that death is not so much a passing on to another life, as the full flowering in grace of this one. Life is not ended, but transformed, transfigured – perfected.

This is the meaning of that last cry of Jesus on the Cross: with a loud voice, he cried: 'It is finished'. The finished work of Calvary is not an ending, but the perfecting of a task given by the Father. The 'loud voice' from the Cross is not a death rattle, but a shout of victory. Scripture scholars say it refers to the Roman officer observing the tide of battle flowing successfully for his troops. As his men would have routed the enemy and secured the last fortress, he would sound the trumpet and shout aloud: 'It is finished'. At that victory sign, the weary soldiers could lay aside their arms and their armour and return home. For John the fight is over. May the Lord grant him rest and victory.

As we remember John who worked and played and fought the battle of life, may we learn ourselves this day to use the gifts and graces entrusted to us. May we know how to make our own homes happy, and how to give place and prepare places for others, so that death may not be an ending, but a finishing touch.

Jesus, you finished the work the Father gave you to do, and your finished work is our salvation. May the offering of this Mass today be an outpouring of that salvation for John. And grant to all here present, the grace to finish the work the Father has given them to do.

*Gabriel Harty OP*

# A Ripe Apple

*Readings:* Prov 31:10-31. Ps 22:1-4. Rom 8:28-30. Mt 25:31-40

A friend of mine, an artist, was preparing a chart for use in teaching religion in school. The chart was for younger children. It was to illustrate the mystery of death. He was puzzled as to how he would design this so he asked his own children what image they would use. He said three were in his mind: three crosses on the hillside of Calvary; leaves falling from a tree; apples falling to the ground in autumn time. His youngest daughter aged seven said: 'I think you should use the apples, Daddy.' He asked, 'Why, darling?' 'Because you can draw faces on the apples.'

The image the little girl suggested was very apt for the passing away of someone so ripe in years as Margaret – because that is how she passed away. She dropped from the tree like a ripe apple – her body fell to the ground but her spirit now soars to eternal life. The image is rich too because it brings out the fruitfulness of her life. Young shoots which sprang from the seed of her life – her children and her grandchildren – were all around her during her long and last illness and were with her at the end. They are with us here now as her mortal body is to be laid in its final resting place.

Some jobs will never be mechanised or computerised or automated, such as the bearing and the rearing of children. This is so because they depend most of all on the human touch, the presence of a loving and caring person. It is that loving touch that we all experienced from our parents from the time we were conceived to the time we left home. And indeed even after that as we remained in contact with our parents. That loving touch has given us inner strength, security and resilience to cope with life's problems.

To withdraw to some extent from the competitive race for honours; to be the quiet back-room person out of the public eye; perhaps to accept and live with a feeling of being unimportant, out of the swing of things; to be 'only a housewife', as some people say; all of that calls for commitment and conviction and a deep-set strength of purpose – to do all of that – and to accept being taken for granted – accept the passage of the years – accept the passage of the image we once held of ourselves – and to continue the daily struggle to mind and provide for growing children – all of that is no easy task. 'When we do the best that we can, we never know what miracle is wrought in our lives or in the life of another.' We do not know what miracles have been worked by the lives of countless parents who gave their all to their families.

Death is the most religious event in our lives. Beside a spirit straining and struggling with life but also reaching out in the vast unknown – into the mystery of God – we come face to face with the veiled presence. Only a thin barrier separates us from him. Then the paper tears. We pass through. If we face this mystery of death with hope and confidence we will also face God and entrust our lives to him. We will let go of everything we think we possess into his hands and let him take care of us.

*Brian Gogan CSSp*

---

## Suggested Alternative Scripture Readings:

Ruth 1:16-17.
Job 8:8-10, 20-21.
Psalms 28:1-2, 6-9. 37:3-9, 16-19. 78:1-7. 85:1-3, 6-8, 12-13. 104:27-32. 112:1-9. 127:1-5. 130.1-8. 133:1-3.
Ecclesiasticus 2:7-13. 3:1-11. 30:4-6.
Daniel 12:1-3.

Acts 10:34-43.
Philippians 3:20-21.

Matthew 5:1-12. 25:31-46.
Mark 15:33-39.

# 3

# Death of a Single Person

## The Spice of Life

*Readings:* Rom 14:7-9. Jn 12:23-28.

The death of a single person is an opportunity to express thanks for a life of generosity and dedication, for service of the church, the local community and families. The rich variety of talents and temperaments in our parish community hints at the richer joys of the kingdom of heaven. We are pilgrims, wayfarers, looking ahead. The marvellous variety of people accompanying us on our pilgrimage offers insights into the nature of God, creator of all, Father of love and mercy.

We all belong to the Lord. He is our origin, our goal, our destiny. This Requiem Mass of Easter hope proclaims how highly God thinks of us. Every person is a valuable person in God's sight. Every person influences others, builds up the community, witnesses to Christ, shares their faith with others. Uncles, aunts, in-laws, neighbours, workmates, cousins, touch us, change us, enrich us, if we are open to accept and appreciate them. All this constant interaction is part of God's plan for the building up of the Body of Christ. Our failures, successes, ups and downs, fit into the pattern of Christ's life.

The Gospel tells the story of an ordinary life. What he did and said often disappointed his countrymen. A failure! they said. The Cross was the prelude to paschal glory. The road that led out from the empty tomb showed the way ahead for humanity. The path to glory begins at the empty tomb, Jerusalem's earth-centre.

Our funeral Mass today celebrates a human life that is changed not ended. We pray, as believers, for a believer in the power of Jesus to save. Recall the words which accompany the baptismal anointing:

As Christ was anointed Priest, Prophet, and King,
so may you live always as a member of his body
sharing everlasting life.

We entrust our friend to the hands of the Lord. A new phase of life has begun. Better things lie ahead. Our friend has passed from our midst into the presence and care of a loving merciful Father, into the realm of the angels and the saints. What we professed in the Creed is now to become a personal experience. What was sown in christening and confirmation approaches fulfilment and fruition.

This prayer of Jesus offered today with his people is powerful and efficacious. The resources of the Church are mobilised to support our departed friend. The blood, sweat and pains of the Saviour cannot have been suffered in vain. They plead for our friend. They are the secure refuge of us who march along the same road. All await the call to pass over to the Lord. 'In him the sadness of death gives way to the bright promise of immortality. Lord, for your faithful people life is changed not ended.' 'Christ is the beginning, the head of the Church; where he has gone, we hope to follow.'

*P J Brophy*

# Good by Stealth

*Readings:* Sir 14:11. 2 Cor 3:1-3

The quality of mourning is somehow different on the death of a priest. It seldom has the raw intimacy that draws forth deep sobs of loneliness. Our memories of the priest often reach so little to the inner heart of him, to the secret springs of character and motive which God alone sees and which God alone judges. And yet there is a serenity to our mourning that finds expression in the Book of Sirach: 'Blessed are those who saw you and were honoured with your friendship' (Sir 14:11).

'Share with all men that Word of God which you have received with joy,' the Bishop invites the young priest on the day of his ordination. Then he lays on him the responsibility to 'see that you believe what you read, teach what you believe and that you translate your teaching into action.' So the priest is called to step forward as a prophet and to speak out from a lived experience of the Gospel. His task is to deliver the message to the men of his time, whether they hear or refuse him a hearing. He must not wrap up his meaning. He must not expect success. The impact of the prophet can seldom be measured by his impact on a single mind here and there but rather by his ability to pierce the hard ring of pride and selfishness that divert so many from following the plan of God for their lives. The mission of the authentic prophet is to tire swimming against the current more often than allow himself to be carried along unconcerned. Just as the prophet's life is different so, often, is his death.

It was said of one eminent churchman that he 'did good by stealth.' Frequently the failings of the priest are more obvious because he is always available for public scrutiny. His good is done by stealth because of the essentially confidential nature of his mission. Occasionally it is only when the priest has died that his largess of compassion comes to light. And that is how he would want it to be because that is the way it was with his master.

Jesus went about 'doing good'. His death, however, was a bitter, lonely affair. His goodness probably only came to light and began to make a universal impact when his first followers reflected on his life and came to write the gospels. It was said of St John of the Cross, one of the church's greatest mystics, that after his death 'people could scarcely remember having met him'.

There are very few statues erected to priests. But there are living

31

statues. Let me explain. In the early Church when there was the danger of half-instructed Christians confusing the minds of the faithful by preaching a spurious gospel, a missionary was expected to carry with him letters of recommendation to prove that he was in good standing. St Paul, speaking to the people of Corinth, told them that 'you yourselves are my letters of introduction, written on your heart to be known and read by all men.' What St Paul was saying was that he was proud of that little group of Christians at Corinth on whom the image of Christ had been stamped through his ministry. They were his credentials. That is the sort of statue that every priest would dearly wish to leave behind. Your fidelity to the faith, as evidenced by your presence here today, is some sign that our brother priest has left an impression, a letter of recommendation written on your hearts.

People in their kindness often say to the priest: 'It's well for you Father, you will go straight to heaven.' The priest winces for he has his own interior struggles, some of them deep and penetrating. Every life that has ended in a position of fidelity to God is a victory. We can join together with our brother to shout: 'I have fought the good fight, I have finished the race.'

*Martin Tierney*

# Sign of Hope

*Reading:* 1 Jn 4:20–5:1

None of us can know what another person's vision of life may be. For some of us, the most important thing is to be married, make a new home, a new family, and leave behind those who will possess a corner of the world in our name. For others it is even more important to do none of these things because there are other, well blessed things which we urgently need to do. In every parish there are heroic people who have never founded a new home or a new family, whose idealism has been of a different kind, whose vision of life has been different from that of many of us. Their way of life and their work has brought blessing on sick people, on old people, on the young who were without other natural help; heroic people who, through the eyes of their faith, saw that it was just as important to care for the old family as it was to found a new one. The love of good people goes to where they see God, however lonely, unusual or difficult the way may be.

'A man who does not love the brother, whom he can see, cannot love God, whom he has never seen. So this is the commandment that he has given us, that anyone who loves God must also love his brother. Whoever believes that Jesus is the Christ has been begotten by God; and whoever loves the Father that begot him loves the child whom he begets' (1 Jn 4:20–5:1).

We do not honour a person because he or she was married, or single, a member of this association or that, but because this is a child of God, who in this life cherished others because they are children of God too; and because God gives to each one of us a vision, a view of life, which is unique and which to some extent we each must follow in a way that is unique. We do not honour the God of infinite resourcefulness by demanding that all his family be exactly the same, doing exactly the same things, having the same vision and the same blessings to give each other. When we pray for idealism we do not ask for one just like our neighbour's; we ask for one unique as only the infinite God can make it unique.

The single person is often for us a sign of hope; standing on the threshold of life, ready to achieve the greatness which only the people of God can experience in God's world; or giving up hope of family and home in order to look for God's people whenever they are in need, to fulfil the ideal of spiritual parenthood. Or simply bearing witness to the power of God which has created such a universe of goodness in a single human soul. *Des Wilson*

33

# Availability

*Reading:* Jn 11:17-27

'I am the resurrection. If anyone believes in me, even though he dies he will live, and whoever lives and believes in me will never die. Do you believe this?' These words have a special significance for all of us who are here today. For some of us they have a uniquely personal significance. We have never heard them in quite the same way before. They challenge us now at a very personal level. 'Do *you* believe this?'

We take nothing or nobody with us when we die. We are on our own. Fathers and mothers, brothers and sisters, wives, husbands, children, friends – all are left behind us. Some leave behind them what we might call a public inheritance – their children, grandchildren, wives or husbands. What others leave behind them is not officially recognised and may be known only to God. We tend indeed to overlook those who live solitary lives. But these were the very ones whom people took for granted. There was the young girl who sacrificed her own prospects in this life to care for aged or ailing parents. And, of course, the prodigal son does not always have so prodigal a father as in the gospel, and in the end he finds himself without wife or child in his old age. There are varieties of gifts and some must travel a lonely road on their pilgrim way.

It happens, though, that often the single aunt or batchelor uncle is the one who is always available to lend a helping hand. They have no children of their own so why should they not help in the minding of other people's children? Why not, indeed? Or, why should they? Who can count the number of Marthas in our midst? Or the Marys who sit at the Lord's feet and listen to his words?

And what role has Lazarus? 'Now Jesus loved Martha and her sister and Lazarus.' Frequently, indeed, it is those who follow this vocation who are always available when a parish needs helpers. And it was Martha who said: 'Yes Lord, I believe that you are the Christ, the Son of God, the one who was to come into this world.' Do you believe this?

*Henry Peel OP*

# Blessed are Those who Mourn

*Reading:* Mt 5:1-12

There is a big temptation not to be personal. But that would be avoiding what is at the heart of our faith. Our personal response to a God who asks of us. Faith isn't real if it isn't mine and it is at moments like this that God calls us at the deepest part of our life. God touches us right at the centre of where we are and who we are.

But what response is he asking of us? He is asking nothing more than the response of love. Nothing more than our sadness, our tears, the pain of the loss that we go through now. That is the most normal, loving response we can make. That is all that our God is asking of us. And he asks us to, to keep on loving, because we know that death does not bring an end to love. If anything it intensifies it. It makes our love much clearer, more vivid. I think that at moments like this, we know that love is eternal. I think that it is for reasons like this that Jesus offers us the promise – 'Blessed are those who mourn'. Our sadness, our tears – they are the measure of the love we have got. The emptiness we feel is the measure of the loss we are undergoing.

So precious is Ted, so real he is now, that we cannot really believe we will not see him again. We cannot really imagine life without him. And that is what we bring to the Lord this morning. So we have got the sadness, the pain and we offer it to him because we have nothing else. We ask him to fill our emptiness with his love. Our tears with his grace. Our fear with his promise.

We bring all this to our Mass this morning with the bread and the wine and we ask the Lord to accept these our prayers, to lead us into his way, his love, his peace. To bring Ted to the life that he promises us all. The life that we all long for. The life that we share. The love and the peace of the Risen Lord. We say with Jesus – 'Happy are those who mourn'. In our prayer we ask him to bring us that happiness. That peace for which we all long.

In the name of the Father
And of the Son
And of the Holy Spirit.
Amen.

*J. Harry Stratton*

# A Loyal Servant

*Reading:* Mt 5:1-11

The funeral of a priest in his own parish is a family affair, and this is entirely as it should be. There should be no more familiar and local person than the parish priest. He can go to any house and find a welcome. He is expected to be a friend to everyone, without distinction, from the least to the greatest, Catholic or non-Catholic, practising or lapsed, old and young. Even though it is unfair and unrealistic, there is a nagging hope that he really can manage to be all things to all men and women. It is his privilege to know and be familiar with so many people; to be able to listen to them, to try to heal them, and to absolve them. He is there to encourage, to laugh, to chide; to teach them, and to pray. It is his calling to represent, to instruct and to guide all the people of God in his parish. He stands up for them against the unjust aggressor; he tries to bring peace between warring parties; he urges people to be reconciled and to forgive. He truly does belong to the family of the parish.

All of us have different memories of him. There are some here who remember him as son, brother, or uncle. We priests knew him as a fellow-priest, a colleague, a friend, a companion. And you remember him as the one who married you, and baptised your children; who buried your loved ones; who celebrated Mass day by day and week by week in your parish. Our memories are fleeting, and somewhat haphazard and disconnected, but they form strangely good patterns, and for all their incompleteness they can be deeply satisfying.

Thank God for the power of memory! This is the *gift* which makes it possible for us to link the past with the present, and be confident about our future. We are here now because we remember, and we are hopeful now because of our memories.

We are in the church which holds in its walls, its graveyard, its registers and in the minds and hearts of the people here, the memory of the whole parish, the whole family – from generation to generation; our memory goes back to the beginning of the parish. And what we are doing is to remember the night that Jesus took bread and wine, said: 'This is my Body; this is my Blood. Do this in memory of me.' Our memory goes back to the Lord Jesus. We do what he did, and in so doing we bring all our own memories to the altar. We bring these memories so that 'they may be acceptable to God the almighty Father'.

Let us realise that the memories we have of another are treasures for our own growth. And now they are held in God's memory. He knows us all through and through, and loves us all with an indescribable love, with complete understanding and compassion. God sees it all – the good, the bad and the patchy bits of our lives; and he still loves us – utterly, totally, unconditionally. For him all that he sees forms a pattern, and while much in the pattern may need forgiving, it is nonetheless a pattern that pleases. Our God is 'all tenderness and compassion, slow to anger, rich in graciousness, and ready to relent' (Joel 2:13).

I believe there is always to be found in a priest who loves his parish – as this man did – one very special quality. It is the quality that is described in one of the Beatitudes: 'Blessed are the pure in heart, they shall see God'. The pure of heart are the completely direct, single-minded, straightforward people. They have a fierce loyalty towards the people they serve. God's love for us is a loyal love; we can be sure that he will never go back on his promise. Your pastor loved you with a loyal love, and whatever failings he may have had, was single-minded in his concern for you. Such purity of heart and will most certainly lead to the vision of God because it is an image – however imperfect – of the love that God has for us. Let us pray for him, as he most surely will for us, that at the end of days we might meet one another merrily in heaven.

+*David Konstant*

37

# Wed to Life

*Reading:* Is 62:2-5

'It is not good for man to be alone.' And the same holds true for woman. Marie was not married in the ordinary sense of the word, but in the deepest and truest sense she was never alone. She was wed to life. Scripture has a quaint expression which speaks of the land of Israel being wed, or being like a wedding dowry. The land of Marie's being was wed by bonds of sacred responsibility and devotion to countless works of charity, and by innumerable hidden services to people and places which heaven alone can record.

Marie was not just a do-gooder – she just loved. How does a single person love? Not for one moment would Marie have thought that the answer lay in her many works of charity, for while she was a worker, she was no workaholic. Never did she refuse to face the individual and the intimate, by drowning herself in a sea of 'busyness'. She knew the difference between serving a need, and answering a call. The sheer daily demand of a parish like ours is so pressing and so vast that to serve all would be an impossibility which might lead to a nervous breakdown, or a guilt complex.

For Marie, the apostolate was a call – a call to love, to grow in the knowledge of the other. This is not to say that she was conglomerate or profligate in her love. True love is an ordered human thing which must have its priorities. St Thomas Aquinas is quite clear: there must be an order in our loving – we love some more than others, and we must begin somewhere.

While Marie might appear to the outer eye to be serving the crying and pressing needs of the day, deep in her spirit she was answering a call – a vocation. Like her Master, she did only the things she saw him do, and responded to the things he told her to do.

This word of explanation is one we may owe to the dead when they can no longer speak for themselves, or, perhaps, even in their lives they were too gentle to reveal all. Love that is responding to a call has often to say 'No'. However good certain works may be, however they may be esteemed, we all have our own calling, our own divine instinct, our own charism. Marie followed her own vocation – maybe at times she followed a distant drum. But she herself respected the different step of the other and was not too troubled if others thought her odd in her ways. Maybe this is the secret of the single person. Call it singularity if you will – but it springs from having a single eye, of being a person unambivalent in God, of being one's own authentic self.

Let us thank God for this grace of the single-eye: amid the passing judgements and the peripheral glances and the squinting eyes, it brings a peace and a poise that is one of life's greatest gifts. Marie had this grace – she carried peace about her as a perfume. And she never became so involved with the good works of God as to neglect the God who apportioned the works and crowned them with fruitfulness. At an early age she had come face to face with the divine humanity of Jesus Christ, and met that sacred humanity head on in all who crossed her path. Her singleness was no escape from love or fruitfulness, for Jesus himself had taught her how to love before his face.

We pray that she may go on for all eternity living and loving before the face of her God and our God, now that this single and singular woman has gone to her wedding.

*Gabriel Harty OP*

# Uncovenanted Love

*Readings:* Dan 3:5ff. Rom 8:19-25. Mt 25:34-40

One of the good things about the Bible is that it offers us a richness that comes in many layers; one layer is that as literature it is both poetic and practical, both tough and comforting, both refined and earthy, both testing and encouraging. Another layer is that, apart from religion altogether, it is the wellspring to which we have spiritual recourse as children of western civilisation. It enshrines our tradition of enlightenment and confronts us with the values that we all inherit. A third layer is that, for those of us who profess Christianity, it is the word of God, bringing us hope through its affirmation of a mysterious but loving God who knows us, searches our hearts and, come what will, keeps us in his unfailing care. Jesus Christ above all discloses in his teaching this: our loving God, all knowing, all beautiful, all merciful.

God's love for us is stronger than death and larger than life. At the end of the day, that love for us is by no means dependent on religious systems, on formularies of theology or on institutional arrangements. God's 'unconvenanted love' is larger than what our limited minds can contain. On our pilgrim way through life we search for meaning and love. This search points towards our mysterious God, as God who may conceal more than he reveals about himself. But God finds us, even if we feel we cannot find him. Pascal's words have the ring of truth about them: 'Oh God, I would not seek you, unless I had already found you.'

Our friend was a good man. He had a large capacity for being affectionate towards his friends. He marvelled at the wonder of nature about him. He enjoyed a strong sense of *dúchas* (of what was natural) and many of us here now recall with gratitude how much we delighted in his company. This morning we give thanks as we pray and believe that he has found rest with God forever.

*Ag Críost an síol. . .*

*Tom Stack*

# Life of Service

*Reading:* Ps 22

It seemed like the ultimate cry of despair. It was a cry of exquisite agony that has echoed down the centuries. How could Jesus cry out in this way at the moment of death? 'My God, my God, why hast thou forsaken me?' Another translation puts it with even deeper pathos: 'O God why have you left me? Why are you so far from me? I can no longer feel you near. I reach desperately for you, but I cannot find you.' The cry of Jesus illustrates the utter helplessness of man against the relentlessness of death. It is convincing evidence of the human-ness of Jesus. The ghastly last question of Jesus emphasises that death can be a time of pain, for the one who is passing away and for those who remain. Jesus was the great High Priest who was like us in all things except sin.

The priest too experiences the pain of living. Sometimes his pain is a suffering with others. Sometimes it is his own. He is a sinner. So often the priest must struggle alone. It is in death that we recognise the fallibility of men just as in death we recognise the humanity of Jesus. Let us forget what might have been and remember our human contact with the deceased. What was the essential fragrance of his character? What were the qualities that will remain in our hearts as seed to inspire and encourage us in the future? There are what appear to be purely human qualities but so often the fruit of these qualities show that they are motivated and inspired by God's Holy Spirit. We thank God for the quality of a life lived for God by our brother.

Jesus said that 'he came to serve'. The priest shares in the priesthood of Christ. His mission is the mission of Christ. It is a mission of service. Above all it is a selfless service. A life given for the people he serves. Jesus acted with compassion and healing in the face of sickness and even death. Today is a day of sadness but the death of a priest is a special time of thanksgiving for a life of service. Remember the nine lepers who never came back to Jesus to thank him for healing them. At the moment of their own deaths they probably regretted their thoughtlessness. They would probably have given anything to have had another opportunity of just saying, 'Thank you, Jesus.' Today we say, quite simply, 'Thank you, Jesus' for the deceased and his service to us.

When Jesus was dying on the cross he was mocked and spat upon; he was jeered. His taunters said mockingly: 'If you are really the Son of God come down from the cross.' And he didn't. His life ended in human failure. But the cross was the highway to the resurrection. He persevered to the end. Had he responded to the tempters and come down from the cross, would there have been a resurrection? The cross is in the centre of the Christian life and it is a cross of victory. When we see the cross in this way then we can proclaim like the preface of the Mass that the sadness of death gives way to the bright promise of immortality.

We have another reason to be thankful today, namely, for the perseverence of the deceased. We know that for your faithful people life is changed not ended. He was a faithful man. His cross, like the cross of Jesus, was one of victory.

*Martin Tierney*

---

*Suggested Alternative Scripture Readings:*

Job 19:23-27.
Psalms 5:1-3, 7-8, 11-12. 15:1-5. 16:1-3, 5-11. 17:1-9, 15. 24:1-6.
    26:1-12 *(Religious)*. 49 *(Poor vagrant)*. 69:1-3, 7;8, 29-34
    *(drowning)*. 116:1-8, 12-17.
Ecclesiasticus 15:1-6. 31:9-11. 34:14-20. 39:1-15 *(Scholar)*.

Romans 5:17-21. 6:3-9. 14:7-12.
Revelation 14:6-7, 12-13. 21:1-7.

Matthew 5:1-12.
Luke 24:13-35.
John 11:17-27.

# 4
## Tragic Death

*Why have You Abandoned Me?*

*Readings:* Lam 3:17-26. Psalm (Lect No 10). Rom 8:14-23.
Jn 11:17-27

There are occasions in life and death which make us cry out 'Why?'
An early or tragic death is one such occasion. Over and above the
grief which we feel on the death of any loved one, there is the extra
and anguished question: why did it have to happen in this way? In
addition to our desolation we feel in some way betrayed by the God
whom we have learned from childhood to call our Father.

All down the ages believers have cried out to God: 'Why have you
allowed this to happen?' Or even more directly: 'Why have you done
this to me?' The psalms are full of cries like these. We must never
hesitate or fear to speak our real feelings to God. He knows them
already, but he also knows our need to express them. His own Son
was forced to cry out to him: 'Why have you abandoned me?' That
cry is part of the mystery of life itself.

Our Father in heaven, as he listens with utmost compassion to our
cry, quietly asks us to believe in and trust him. He does not 'send'
these crosses which pin us to the ground. They come to us, as they
come to God's own Son, from the conditions of life in this world,
and they come to us unbidden and unwanted as occasions for deep
and anguished faith. God does not explain why these demands are
made of us and even if he did, we would not be able to understand.
Such answers belong to the end of time when earth and sea will have
yielded up their dead, when their will be no more sorrow and pain,
and when God will wipe away all tears. In the meantime he asks us
to offer him the weight of our grief and the sacrifice of our tears and
he will support us. He asks us for faith and trust at the very moment
when we feel that we have none to offer him. He is never nearer than
when we are drained of all feeling and incapable of seeing clearly
enough to pray. It is when we feel that we have nothing else left to
offer him but our emptiness and desolation that his Spirit approaches
us most nearly. 'Even though he slay me, yet will I trust him' is an
old and tested prayer. Many men and women have used it when they

43

were near despair and through it have come to know more about God's love than others who have been less tried or afflicted in lesser ways.

There is a kind of divine helplessness which is really divine strength. God's purposes are being slowly and painfully worked out in this world of ours in ways which surpass our power to understand. He does not will an early or a tragic death, but such deaths happen in the world he is creating. And when they do, he is there with his plea that we should trust and love him, that we should believe in his Spirit of consolation who enfolds us in his loving arms, and that from all this grief and pain he will draw an immense happiness and glory for the future.

That is why he sent his Son into our world. That is why he watched his Son die in agony of mind and body, so that we might know that he knows from the inside what it means to suffer, to grieve, and to experience the deepest desolation. We are all part of the mystery of God's creation and of his purposes. Our faith tells us that in spite of the darkness we are sometimes called upon to enter on our journey through life, the road will end in the triumph of light and joy and final meaning of it all.

*Gabriel Daly OSA*

# More Ready than They Knew

*Reading:* Lk 12:38

We are here because in the second watch of last Friday night forty-eight young people died suddenly, tragically, and in a way that leaves all of us feeling numb and helpless. 'Happy are those whom he finds ready.' The Gospel words seem unreal. So many of them could not have been ready – they were too young. Too young to take death seriously. They had not time to know their way in life. Many of them must have been unsure of many things – unsure of themselves, unsure of where life was leading, unsure of God. At sixteen or seventeen or even more, it was too soon to be ready, to have everything together for that journey.

A dying women in hospital quite low in herself and in considerable pain said: 'It's so alone and pointless,' but then she added: 'Father, all my life I've tried to do my best in everything.' And I replied to her: 'I only ask to be able to say the same when my times comes.' Talking things over she found she was more ready then she knew, more ready than she imagined. And we pray that the same be true for those many killed on Friday night, that they may be more ready than they knew. It was too soon to be ready in understanding, in commitment, in wisdom. But they could be ready in heart and in hope – just by trying to do their best in all the explorings of their growing, and in the everyday school of love.

What does death do to life? A famous answer was given centuries ago by John Donne: 'No man is an island. Any man's death diminishes me because I am involved in mankind, and therefore never send to know for whom the bell tolls, it tolls for thee.' I would suggest a simpler answer still. I think death makes life precious because today might not have been, and today will never come again. Death makes life urgent for love. So for us here another word of that same twelfth chapter of St Luke may speak and challenge: to whom more is given – more life, more time, more chances for wisdom and service – from them much more is required. As John Donne would say, a moment of disaster, such as we now experience so intensely, is a powerful intimation of mortality. But it is also an invitation to thanksgiving for what we are given, and a moment to re-focus our lives in prayer towards what really matters.

*Michael Paul Gallagher SJ*

# *Waiting in Hope*

*Readings:* Lam 3:17-26. Lk 25:13-35

Unexpected death hits all of us, with appalling suddenness. We still cannot fully take in the reality even as we carry out funeral rites. We feel the sort of shocked confusion that the two disciples in the Gospel account felt: 'We had hoped. . .,' they said. We also had hoped, and even taken for granted, all sorts of things. (S)he had a place in many of our plans and expectations. Like the disciples, we do not understand, yet like them, we want somehow to hope. We can still hope. They had to learn that the overturning of their plans and expectations, even the death of the person on whom they had pinned so many hopes, was not the end of everything.

God's ways are not our ways. He calls us along paths we would never have chosen. Jesus foretold the death of St Peter by telling him, 'Another will gird you and carry you where you do not wish to go' (Jn 21:18). It was necessary that even the Christ should suffer. Because God's plans are greater than ours, they sometimes shatter our expectations. At times like this we feel helpless, 'bereft of peace', we 'have forgotten what happiness is.' And yet in the darkness, we remember that 'the steadfast love of the Lord never ceases' (Lam 3). We are helpless in the face of death; in that helplessness we see clearly the fragility of our expectations. If everything depended on what we could achieve and what we could ensure, we would be lost. There are tragedies, like this death, which we can do nothing to prevent. Still we believe that God's love never ceases and we can still hope.

We are people who wait. We wait for what God will do in his own way and at his own time. We wait in confusion and bewilderment and grief, but we wait in hope. Even the suffering of Christ was necessary. The disciples could not understand it; we cannot understand either. We wait, knowing that we will never fully understand until we are reunited with the deceased and with one another in the glory of Christ.

> 'The Lord is good to those who wait for him, to the soul that seeks him. It is good that one should wait quietly for the salvation of the Lord' (Lam 3).

+*Donal Murray*

46

# Allotted Time

*Reading:* Qo 3:1-9

Death is a fact of life. It is part of the mystery of life. One of the most disturbing aspects of death, once we accept its inevitability, is that it seems to be both *blind* and *deaf;* blind in not looking to see if its victim is young or old, healthy or weak, productive or not; deaf in that it doesn't hear our cries for just a little more time to live, to straighten out our affairs, to do all the tomorrow things our todays left undone.

I believe that when I die, I will look back down through the corridor of time, and see quite clearly that every single thing that happened to me in life had a potential for great good for me, whether I saw it that way or not at the time, or whether I made use of it or wasted it. This hindsight could very well include the timing and circumstances of my death, when I will see clearly that even this was for my own good. I believe that part of the mystery of life and death is that there *is* a time for everything under heaven, that the Lord of the harvest never plucks a flower from the garden of life without first ensuring that it has completed its allotted time there.

Sometimes, when a peson dies suddenly or tragically, there is the often-unspoken question in the minds of the bereaved: 'I wonder was he ready?' The church's teaching, or theology of death, is quite specific on this. No one is lost or saved simply because chance so brought it about, because he was suddenly snatched off into eternity. No, God is not small-minded, and he is infinitely just. Many of our theologians, Rahner, Boros, Troisfontaines, for example, teach that, at the moment of death, when I am free from the prison of the body, when with blinding clarity, I can see myself in relationship to God, others, and all of the universe, I shall encounter Christ personally, and, even at this late stage, make a fundamental decision to accept or reject him. God does not *send* us anywhere when we die. He eternalises whatever decision we make. Jesus is the *only* door to the sheep-fold (Jn 10:7). 'No one comes to the Father but by me,' he tells us (Jn 14:6).

Two thirds of the people of the world will die and never have heard of Jesus. If justice is to be done, they must be given an opportunity in death for the greatest decision of all. Like the owner of the vineyard that Jesus tells us about, who gave the same wages to those who came along at the last minute as he gave to those who had been in the vineyard all day, we should, indeed, be grateful that God doesn't do things our way! I myself believe that justice is also seen to be done at this point for those who have been called away without any warning or specific preparation. We are dealing here with a tender loving Father, with a capacity for love and forgiveness away beyond the ability of us mere mortals to appreciate. Fr Bede Jarrett, the famous Dominican preacher, said in Hyde Park, London, one time: 'When I die, I would much prefer to be judged by God than by my own mother.'

When death is sudden, unexpected, or tragic, it is the bereaved who are at the centre of the tragedy, and who suffer from the suddenness. Not only have they *lost* someone, but they themselves can feel quite lost. There is no short-cut, no *safe* short-cut, through bereavement. Death doesn't end a relationship. In the first birth the cord is cut that bound the child to the mother. The relationship is not ended, it has moved into a newer phase. It's the same when the cord binding a person to this life is cut, and someone belonging to us has moved on into the fullness of life. Time, and the love and support of our friends, together with our trust in a loving Father's plan, all of these carry us through to the quiet conviction and certain hope of a resurrection and unending life together.

*Jack McArdle SS CC*

# They Crucified Him

*Reading:* Mk 15:25

A famous theologian once advised preachers not to console where there is no scope for consolation, not to give simple solutions to life's problems when their ultimate solution lies in God's incomprehensibility, his nature and his freedom.

Once I was sitting down near a huge crucifixion scene in front of an American college when a young lady came up and exclaimed: 'Couldn't they have put up a nicer crucifixion?' Quietly I began to tell her about the dreadful violence of the crucifixion which was perpetrated on the good Jesus; how we have domesticated the crucifixion. Can you imagine wearing or putting up a hangman's noose or an electric chair? The cross is the symbol of man's inhumanity to man, a symbol which is simultaneously the sign of the greater love of God himself for man. In a crucifixion no vital artery was pierced. Its purpose was to prolong the hunger, thirst, disgrace and agony of the sufferer as long as possible. The unfortunate victim was provided with a small seat to bear his weight so as to prevent his collapse and prolong the agony. And all this happened to Jesus.

We wrestle with the meaning of suffering, especially senseless, violent suffering, all our lives. Agnostics tend to see the senseless suffering of innocent people, symbolized by Jesus' own crucifixion, as proof that a caring God does not exist. Perhaps, like the popular songwriter, we are tempted even to blasphemy at the senseless suffering of the world and insist that:

> It is God they ought to crucify,
> Instead of you and me,
> I said to the carpenter
> A-hanging on the tree.

The story of the cross as Paul gradually realised, is one of foolishness, a stumbling block both to the pious Jew and the cultured Gentile alike. But to those who make the leap of faith it is the power and the wisdom of God. The realisation that it was God whom they (or rather 'we') crucified brings a whole new perspective to the suffering of the world. The cross interprets what happens to the oppressed and marginalised of the world, to the victims of our society whose list seems endless. It does not provide the simple neat explanation which we would like. But it reminds us that our God lived and died in solidarity with the victims rather than the successful

49

of our society, that our God was foolish enough to become one with those who suffer and die. Among those who are abandoned and forsaken we can expect to find the healing presence, the hopeful power of our God.

Jesus, according to some theologian, could have saved us 'by twiddling his thumbs'. But how little such an act would have shown of God's care for man in his freedom, his greatness and his misery. God did not make Jesus die because his 'justice' demanded it. He entered our experience to share from within what it means to live, to suffer, and to die. Jesus helps us to find meaning and hope in our sufferings, to discover love at the heart of things. The question is not why does God let people suffer but why does he let himself suffer in Jesus.

The test of religion is this capacity to help us cope with the unfairness, even the absurdities, of life. The cross of Jesus stands poised between heaven and earth, his body stretched out in all four directions, his arms reaching out to embrace all sufferers. It is a cruel reminder of the harsh reality of life from which we all try to escape in our illusion, our political systems, our wisdom. But above all it speaks to us of the deeper, higher things, of hope and love at the heart of the universe. Even though the vast seas seem often violent and disturbed to us yet this disturbance is only on the surface of the mighty deep.

*Sean P Kealy CSSp*

# God's Instruments

*Reading:* Jn 10:14-15

It is our Christian custom to make a joyful occasion when our friends die. It is a quiet joy, which brings tears just as any overwhelmingly joyful event during our lifetime brings tears. At the death of our friends we think of the tears as natural and becoming; we tend to hide the joy. Yet the funeral celebration recalls the most joyful of events – the creation, the renewal and the inspiration by God, the Father, Son and Holy Spirit, of his people. Even when we have killed some of our friends, we do not meet in Christian worship in order to condemn those who killed or praise the association to which the dead belonged. We come to remember those three things which no human association can damage, or enhance: creation by the Father, renewal by the Son, inspiration of the Holy Spirit. With such mighty gifts as these a human being can only be to a most trifling degree either enhanced or degraded by any of our human associations.

If we were wise we would thank God that once again God's good judgement will triumph over the most evil judgement we can make. And every soul sent on before its time places on us an obligation to cherish and save another life; our return for killing is not to kill again but to save. Man's vengeance becomes God's instrument of forgiveness and reparation. Just as Jesus had his harvest in death, so do his followers:

> I tell you, unless a wheat grain falls on the ground and dies, it remains only a single; but if it dies, it yields a rich harvest'
> (Jn 12:24).

We do not wish the untimely death of our friends, but we recognise God's message in it when it comes.

We live in a frighteningly hostile environment. We could die, not from disease, not from violence, not by accident, but simply from exposure. From exposure, so hostile is the environment that just to be exposed to it would kill us. God for his own good purposes, which we cannot pretend to explain, has created his world that way. Our greatest shame is that we have made the environment even more hostile by our unnecessary antagonisms, our wars, our dangerous games. If we were to use every resource we had to make our friends safe in this world, what an immense and worthwhile task that would be. It would take all our strength, courage and wealth. But with work like that, well done, behind us, we would never fear death ourselves.

Our Lord's words about being the good shepherd are remembered especially at the death of our friends. In speaking as he did he was celebrating the greatest goodness that any person can achieve to preserve, cherish and protect the rich life which God, the Father, Son and Holy Spirit, has given us:

> I have come so that they may have life and have it to the full. I am the good shepherd; the good shepherd is one who lays down his life for his sheep (Jn 10:14-15).
>
> A woman in childbirth suffers, because her time has come: but when she has given birth to the child she forgets the suffering in her joy that a man has been born into the world (Jn 16:21).

The response of Jesus Christ our Lord to suffering and death is a divine love of new life. That is our joyful response too.

*Des Wilson*

# Jesus Shared our Life and our Death

*Readings:* Rom 8:31-35,37-39. Psalm: *How gracious is the Lord, and just.* Mk 15:33, 16:1-6

In death as in life our aim is to imitate Christ. And this is a reality. The Son of God shared our human life. Saint Paul says he 'emptied himself of his glory'. From the smelly straw of the stable of Bethlehem to the hard wood of the Roman cross, Jesus lived a human life to the full. Like us in all things but sin. Even there he took on himself its burden. The Son of Glory imprisoned himself in time and place. St John says: 'The Word became a human being and lived among us.' In learning to live like him we mingle spiritually with his companions and friends. We meet the real people he encountered, fishermen, farmers, shepherds, religion teachers, Roman soldiers, unfortunates of all kinds of mind and body. We can sit in on his interviews, with Nicodemus, the blind man, the Samaritan woman. We move freely from our situation into his backgrounds of desert, mountains, lakes, villages and city. It is familiar territory. Human beings do not change much across time and place.

Jesus shared our life and set an example for us. He also shared our death. Of all the turning points in our life, death is the ultimate one, a crisis. We see our Lord at grips with death, the widow's only son, the twelve-year-old daughter of Jairus, his friend Lazarus. All very moving. Jesus was so moved at the death of Lazarus that he wept with Mary and the Jews. Faced with grief on these occasions he substitutes the word 'sleep' for the harsher word 'death'. Deeper than sorrow is hope and joy, and a note of glory and triumph:

> Now my heart is troubled; and what shall I say? Shall I say: 'Father, do not let this hour come upon me?' But that is why I came, to go through this. O Father, bring glory to your name.' Then a voice spoke from heaven: 'I have brought glory to it, and I will do so again' (Jn 12:27-28).

As human beings we struggle with the problems of sickness, suffering, tragedies, wars, disasters, and sin. We also come to grips with death. And we often ask 'why?' Why should an innocent little child die in its cot? Why should a young man die tragically in the bloom of life? Why the death of the mother of a large family? St Paul has an answer for us. 'God did not spare his own Son but gave him up to benefit us all.'

Suffering and death are mysterious. Our questions will continue.

But we know that love is stronger than death. It may seem that God has abandoned the sufferer, but we triumph by our trials. Further, it is a privilege to share in the redeeming sufferings of Christ. What a strange teaching. To die is to sleep. From poisonous wounds come healing. Glory transfigures the bloodstained crucified face. 'My God, my God, why have you forsaken me?' The suffering servant wins the deliverance of the nations. It must be that God who gave his only Son understands tragedy. His own Son was a victim of violence. All victims, young and old, are gathered into the bosom of God.

The angels hailed the birth of Jesus in the poor stable of Bethlehem. His human life meant the kingdom of God, faith, hope, and love, the good news of salvation. He was obedient to the will of his Father even to the death on the cross. For our sake he opened his arms on the cross. An embrace. God did not abandon him. As in the beginning an angel is there again. A young man in white robe hailing victory: 'He has been raised'. This triumphant risen Lord stands at the right hand of God and pleads for us, pleads for our liberation from sin and death, from hatred, pain, sorrow, tragedy.

Who then can separate us from the love of Christ? Can trouble do it, or hardship, or persecution, or hunger, or danger or death? No, in all these things we have complete victory through him who loved us!

*Raymond Murray*

54

# Sudden Death, Sudden Mercy

*Readings:* Rom 6:3-4,8-9. Jn 11:27-31

Frequently in church the celebrant invites us to stir up our faith when he says: 'The Lord be with you.' We get the message. We all want God's blessing on what we plan and do. St Patrick urges us to have Christ with us always. Our life as Christians began at baptism. The Lord came to us to stay with us. Christening is a resource event which we can return to as often as we please, and to our enrichment. We are signed, sealed and delivered into the arms of Mother Church. Water and oil was poured, light and clothing were given to us for our pilgrim journey to the Father.

We receive the candle, the light of Christ to show us how to nourish the divine life infused into us. On our behalf, parents and godparents say 'yes' for us to loving and serving God. The white christening robe spoke of our dignity as Christians. Good things followed. The Church as Mother did not fail us with provisions for our needs. Confirmation, confession, communion, the Sunday Eucharist, the parish community of faith, the experience of prayer at home, in church, at odd moments of the day, the word of God for our guidance, the teaching of the Church for our instruction. We grew into the family of God. We enjoyed fellowship and knew we belonged and were loved. Church membership is a grace, a gift, a blessing.

'Lord, if you had been here my brother would not have died,' said Martha. But Jesus is here. Jesus never abandons his people. Home is where you belong. Home is where they have to let you in when you return.

A life has ended suddenly. Jesus was there. God is faithful. Jesus is the pledge of God's fidelity. The life that has ended its earthly phase is a life dear to God, treasured by Christ, sealed with the sufferings and pains of Calvary. One so deeply loved by God will always be loved and be present to the Father of mercy. God does not withdraw his love.

Now confronted with the unexpected, we cry out: 'Mercy Lord. Increase our faith. You are the resurrection and the Life. . . Whoever believes and lives in you will never die.' God does not fail his people in life nor in death. The resources of the church are adequate to cope with every crisis in the life of the person and of the family. The help of God is nearer than the door. God reaches out to help and sustain all who pass through the gates of death and approach their true homeland.

Sudden death, sudden mercy, says the voice of faith. The God who nevers fails his people in life will most certainly be their sure support in death sudden or accidental.

Lord, strengthen our faith. Deepen our understanding of your great love. Your love for the one we mourn is deeper than ours. Lead him safely home to be with you for ever.

*P J Brophy*

---

*Suggested Alternative Scripture Readings:*

Psalms 30:1-12. 56:3-4, 10-13. 61:1-2, 5-9, 11-12. 65:1-5. 108:10-13.
Wisdom 3:1-9.
Isaiah 25:6-9.

Romans 8:31-39.
1 Corinthians 15:51-57.
1 John 3:14-16.
Revelation 12:10-12. 20:11-12. 21:1-4.

Matthew 25:1-13.
Luke 12:35-40.
John 17:24-26.

# 5
## Death After a Long Illness

## Silent Witness

Readings: 25:6-9. Lam 3:17-26. Mt 11:25-30

Jesus Christ set a headline for his followers in the life of service of others that he led. He went about doing good, doing the will of his Father. His first concern was for the sick and the handicapped. He went to them. They were attracted to him. The man who waited patiently by the pool Probatica could hardly believe his good fortune. Jesus raised him, rewarding his faith and patience. In curing the sick Jesus showed that God cares, that God is aware of his suffering servants. The life of Jesus is one of patient service, duplicated time after time in the sick.

Illness is a form of service, a lonely witness to weakness, to helplessness, isolation and pain. There is a great mystery about illness. Isaiah looked forward and saw in the Messiah one who was the prototypal man of sorrows and acquainted with grief. Jesus was often fatigued but we never hear that he was ill. His life of total self-giving to his Father and to his own people in Palestine ended in humiliation, pain, desolation and crucifixion.

The silent witness of patient suffering is a challenge to mankind to enter into the deepest meaning of life. Waiting on God can be a wearying process. The bondage of illness has its compensations in insight into forms of service and fidelity.

Jesus is the one who sets us free from enslavement to what is not of God. The redemptive value of suffering is mysterious and is appreciated only under the inspiration of the Spirit who gives courage and generosity. Christ is the medicine of the heavenly Father, true physician of human health, says a Spanish ritual.

Lord of hosts, consoler of those who mourn, defender of those who are prostrated, console in your goodness those who are captives of their sorrow for the deceased. Heal all the pain in their hearts. Grant rest in the bosom of Abraham to your servant who has fallen asleep in the hope of the resurrection to eternal life. Wipe away all tears and flood with joy the heart that has been purified by the trials of a long illness.                                                    *P J Brophy*

# A Great Relief

*Reading:* Ps 103

When someone dies after a long, painful illness we often hear it said: 'It's a great relief.' And this is intended to apply to both the person who has died, and to those who have looked after the deceased. For those who believe in eternal life in Christ, then it makes great sense to say that, because we understand that the dead person has exchanged his life of pain for a life of happiness, increased through the way the dead person coped with his or her suffering before death.

If they have had a deep sense of their creaturehood all during their lives, they will more easily be able to accept the consequences of their fragility and limitation, which is so deeply experienced in sickness. Acceptance in as full a positive sense as possible leads to even greater maturity, cleansing the person of everything but concern for what is of ultimate importance. Acceptance is a personal act, an active one, rather than merely passive.

Coping in faith with suffering produces strength of character. This does not make it any the less painful, but it is not wasted, and prepares the sick person for a future that is one he accepts and chooses, rather than one he detests and resents. Suffering that is not accepted is a waste and destructive. Suffering that is accepted can lead to profit and be a real contribution to the task of preserving and developing the nobility of the human person.

Death will be seen, not only as a release from pain, but also as a peaceful and gentle passage into the hands of the welcoming and smiling Christ, who knows from his own personal experience what it is to suffer.

The Christian who has suffered long, and who has died in peace and with dignity, has lived the Gospel. His/her funeral is a celebration of the power of the grace of God, and a dramatic message to all of how to be truly human, of how to rise to the challenge of illness in ways that are enriching and life-giving, and above all a proclamation that the human being's real life is with God in eternal happiness. From illness accepted with human dignity we all learn to live in the perspective of God's kingdom.

*Michael Mulvihill CSSp*

# Chosen Souls

*Reading:* Mt 9:18-22

Jesus invites us to follow him, and he promises to bring us home. He never said it would be easy, because the road he walked was not easy. He *did* say, of course, that those who follow him would not walk in darkness, but would have the light of life. To follow him means taking up our own cross, whatever that may be. Someone said one time that the greatest man that ever walked this earth was given a cross, and if you're lucky, you will get one too!

There is a difference between sickness and suffering. Not all sickness is sent by God, nor is all sickness necessarily suffering. Suffering is a vocation, it is redemptive, it is a direct sharing in the suffering of Jesus. Only chosen souls are called to the ministry and apostolate of suffering. If my eyes cannot see, then my hands and ears have to do my seeing for me. It is the same in the Body of God's people. In a pleasure seeking, hedonistic society, where many people avoid pain at all costs, where drugs of all kinds are used to deaden the realities of life, then someone in the Body must carry the cross. I believe there are many such chosen souls around, in our hospitals, or suffering in their homes, who are carrying the cross for the rest of us. The vocation of suffering is accompanied by the grace and strength to carry the cross, and the sufferer is redeemed and purified in the process.

If you are a Christian, you are expected to do your dying during your *life-time*. Dying during my life-time is the dying that is required if I am to live the Christian life, dying to my own self, my self-sufficiency, my independence, all of which can be part of a long illness. There is a *real* dying here, and usually when the end comes there's a quiet slipping away, because the dying has taken place long ago.

When we are dealing with people who have had a long journey of illness, we have to think of *their* needs too. A child frequently falls asleep protesting that he is not tired. He vainly fights to stay awake. A sleepy person needs to sleep, *a dying person needs to die*. Death can be as natural as sleep. There comes a time when it is unreasonable, as well as useless, to resist either sleep or death. The bereaved have to deal with this resistance too. We don't really begrudge them their rest, but we do feel deprived of their companionship.

We are people of hope, of an eternal hope. Another member of the family has gone home, while we are left to plod along through the valley of life for another while. It is a bit like when you and your family and friends go out for a walk in the park or the woods, and one goes on ahead, and out of sight, perhaps around the corner, or over the brow of the hill. As Pope John XXIII used to say: 'Dead? They're not dead; they've gone home, just around the corner; they're waiting for you.' Fr Bede Jarrett OP says: 'Death is only an horizon, and an horizon is nothing but the limit of our sight.'

There is an old Irish saying: 'Death is the poor man's best doctor.' For a person who has endured prolonged illness, death can, indeed, be a very real healing. Indeed, death is the total healing of all of our human ills. The Lord's death is the total healing of all of our human ills. The Lord's healing hand has reached out to touch the deceased and now he is well again.

*Jack McArdle SS CC*

# A Blessed Mourning

*Reading:* Mt 5:1-12

Our Lord has just said to us: 'How happy are those who mourn.' That is a very strange thing to say. Nobody else ever said anything like that. But then 'never did any man speak as this man speaks'. If we are to grasp what it means we must first of all accept it in faith. Our Lord said it so it must be true.

It is through listening to our Lord, believing in his word, that understanding dawns. Our mourning is not futile. It is not meaningless. It is not a wild cry of despair. We believe this because our Lord tells us so. It is he himself who gives significance to all our sorrows. He tells us that there is blessedness in our pain. That is a great comfort when life is painful.

Pain forms part of every human life. Our Saviour teaches us that pain is part of the process of redemption. All good Christians know this. I remember once at Lourdes talking to an invalid. She said to me: 'Father, I don't mind now if I am never cured.' She had found a joy that was deeper than any pain. The Mother of God, who stood by the cross of her son, had brought this understanding. When the shadow of the cross falls on us we are in good company.

We mourn for those whom we love. So our mourning is a sign of our love. We have been privileged to have had what is most precious in human life. Our mourning signifies our privilege. Those who have never loved will never mourn. Their hearts will never be broken. And so they are the most deprived people on earth. They have missed what makes life worthwhile. How blessed are those who mourn.

But we do not mourn as those who are without hope. Love is stronger than death. Love abides forever. All partings are painful. When our Lord was preparing his disciples for the time when he would be taken away from them, he said that he was going to prepare a place for them. 'And if I go,' he said, 'I will come again and take you to myself that where I am you may be also.'

We pray today that our friends who have been taken from us have been taken by our Lord to be at home with him where death will be no more, no mourning, nor crying, nor any sorrow. We pray that all of us may one day come to be at home with the Lord forever.

*Henry Peel OP*

# May Eternal Light

*Readings:* 2 Cor 4:5-16. Jn 12:44-50

When a Christian dies a light goes out. Every Christian reflects in and to the world in which he lives something of the light of Christ, that light which we long for and pray for in the poignant Advent liturgy.

> Christ the sun, all sloth expelling
> shines upon the morning skies.

Christ the Daystar appearing in a world of darkness and sin. The light which is Christ is in turn reflected in the Church which is Christ on this earth and the individual Christian assimilates, borrows and makes his own something of that light, which is reflected for him in the domestic Church, his own family, in the local Church. And that light which shines in the life of the Christian and which reveals Christ to others takes on various expressions, various tints and hues depending on the mood of the moment. There is the bright light of hope, the glowing light of love and the intense light of a moment of great joy. There are times too when that light takes on a somber mood, begins to flicker when the going gets tough and one is buffeted by the storms and stresses of life.

But there are in our world some extraordinary men and women who somehow or other manage to keep the light aflame no matter how taxing the trial or the burden of affliction that weighs upon them. And that is how I would like to remember the deceased. I have never seen him in a bad humour. Even when his pain was considerable and his strength was ebbing there was always the smile and the twinkle which indicated that he knew that you knew but he wasn't going to embarrass you by referring to it. But it was all of a piece with the rest of his life. He was a happy man, his was the great Christian virtue of contentment. He found joy in such simple things as tending to his garden, taking his family for a drive on a Sunday, visiting his country relatives, sailing his blue boat on the Shannon, which was his pride and joy, paying a visit to the local with a few very intimate friends who are here today and who stood by him until the end.

We pray that he has gone into the possession of eternal light, into that City whose day knows no dimming, and whose sun knows no setting for the glory of God is its light, and its lamp is the lamb.

*Eltin Griffin OCarm*

# *Easter Person*

*Reading:* Jn 14

> If you love me you will keep my commandments.
> I shall ask the Father and he will give you another Advocate. . .
> I will not leave you orphans – I will come back to you.
> In a short time, the world will no longer see me,
> because I live and you will live.

The reading is all about life – about abundant life – about the life that has already conquered death. Joan had a long and painful illness, and some might say her death was a happy release: she has gone home. Yet that is not the whole truth, for Joan was always at home with God.

Many years back this brave girl sensed in her own heart, as well as from the words of her doctors, that she might have a long spell as an invalid. How could she face it? Like many another she discovered that it is possible to accept any *how* if one has a *why?* She found her way through, in the words of this day's Gospel: 'I will not leave you orphans, I will come back to you.' Joan accepted those words with all the immediacy, with all the here and now significance which St John had given them. She was not waiting for death and judgement to meet Jesus. She had learnt how to open herself to him right where she was, and he had come to her just as he had promised. Her long illness had been no isolation from life – for she had found the fullness of life in a Jesus who was *now*. She had found the secret of laying claim to the promises of Christ and she expected them to be fulfilled.

And his words were:

> I will not leave you orphans,
> I will come back to you. . .

And she remembered that he promised to come back 'soon', 'in a little while'. For Joan then there was no looking to a dim distant future. Resurrection was no 'sleep-in' for the future. She had already begun to live the life of the new creation. She knew what it meant to be an Easter-person, even in the Lent of life. The words of the French writer, Camus, come to mind:

> Don't walk before me, I may not follow,
> Don't walk behind me, I may not lead;
> Just walk beside me and be my friend.

Joan had discovered something of the 'Closer Walk with Jesus', indeed that lovely old hymn was often on her lips. And that walk led her to the 'Inner Land' flowing with milk and honey. Like so many who are confined physically, she wandered freely through the country of the spirit. Prayer and intimacy with Jesus led her through, until she found the inner land of her own being. There she could be free as the wind; there above all she could be master – and there she could invite Jesus to come, to live with her, to love her, to reign over her.

Death came, then, not simply as an end, but as the conquest of a promised land. She never thought in terms of corpses and coffins and cemeteries, but in terms of life and love and land. Death was for Joan the great voyage of discovery. 'All I want,' she said, 'is what my heart and my soul are straining for: to let go and to let Jesus come.' That coming was a daily event in the life of Joan. Her end was a daily beginning. Death was not the coming of a stranger from afar, but an intimate companion, who took her by the hand and said:

> Arise, make haste my love, my dove, my beautiful one and come.
> The winter is over and gone;
> the flowers have appeared in our land,
> the time for singing has come.
> (Canticle of Canticles/Song of Songs)

*Gabriel Harty OP*

# The Final Healing

*Readings:* Ps 41:2, 3, 5; 42:3-5. Jn 11:3-6, 11-12. Mt 5:1-12.

The mystery of death is cruel, sudden, final, irrevocable, absurd, savage. It can make everything that goes before in life appear a sham. If we dwell on it, it can take all meaning, hope and joy out of life. When someone we love dies, it can be the last straw. It can make what is in many ways a cruel, savage and grotesquely unjust world seem a hundred times worse. At times we can ignore this as we are caught up in the activities of life. At other times, such as the sudden loss of a loved one, the whole universe can seem a ruthless, unwelcoming place.

The world is a contradictory place. There is so much wonder in it, so much splendour in it, so much enjoyment and pleasure, on the one hand. On the other hand, one is bedevilled by the sight of poverty which destroys human lives; disease which frustrates the happiness of thousands; hunger and want which afflict multitudes; the threat of war and disaster and constant violence which turns a garden of paradise into a valley of death. How can all this suffering, all this agony, all this darkness be reconciled with the God who claims he is a God of love, of mercy and of friendship?

It is in the resurrection of Christ and his promise of resurrection for us that this dilemma is resolved. The contradiction between sadness and joy, hunger and plenty, disease and well being, decreptitude and wholeness, war and peace is resolved for me in the mystery of the resurrection. The world is caught up in an evolutionary process – from that great primeval bang which began it all, to the final moment when all is revealed and we can all see God face to face. This evolutionary process is not crowned by cybernetic, electronic or optical technology. Its final point and its completion is the transformation of death. It is when death gives way to life, eternal life, that the evolution of the universe and of the individual human person is complete. When death is not the end but the beginning, then we can begin to see the face of God even behind the disasters which surround us. The hope of resurrection changes the equation. It turns recession and depletion into perfect health, bankruptcy into infinite riches.

In this vision of human life, then, death is not the failure of therapy but the final healing. It is not a closed door but a threshold to a world where all tears are wiped away and our hearts are filled with unlimited joy. As the poet has put it: 'Death is blowing out the candle because the dawn has arrived.' As the caterpillar dies the butterfly flies off into the sun. And that is our hope for all our friends who die, and indeed for ourselves that as we shed this mortal body, we are clothed in the new spiritual body of the resurrection. And we follow Christ, the first born of many brethren, into that place of unending peace. His promise is that when we get there, everything we have suffered or borne in this life will appear as nothing. Or as he put it so eloquently in his discourse at the Last Supper: 'When a woman is in travail, she has sorrow because her hour has come; when she is delivered of the child, she no longer remembers the anguish, for joy that a child is born into the world. So you have sorrow now, but I will see you again and your hearts will rejoice, and no one will take your joy away from you!'

*Brian Gogan CSSp*

---

## *Suggested Alternative Scripture Readings:*

Job 33:19-26.

Psalms 6:1-7. 13:1-5. 18:1-6. 22:1-5, 9-11, 14-15. 25:15-18, 20-21. 30:1-12. 31:1-5, 7-10, 12, 14-16, 19-22. 32:1-7. 38:1-2, 7-10, 13-15, 21-22. 41:1-3, 10-13. 42:1-4. 43:3-5. 55:1-2, 4-9, 22. 61:1-8. 63:1-8. 73:21-28. 102:1-5, 9-11, 18-20. 109:24-27, 30-31. 119:45-50, 74-77, 153-154, 175-176.

Ecclesiasticus 40:1-7, 11.

Romans 5:5-11. 8:14-23. 8:31-39.
1 Corinthians 15:51-57.
2 Timothy 2:8-13.
1 John 3:14-16.
Revelation 2:9-12. 12:10-12. 20:11-12. 21:1-4.

Matthew 5:1-12.

# 6

# Death of a Handicapped Person

## *The Inner Man*

*Readings:* Wis 9:13-16. 2 Cor 4:16-18

We thank God for the differences between us. We do not understand the reason for them; often we cannot cope with them. It is easy to decide that most of us are what human beings should be, and that there are a few who are so different that they must be called deprived, or handicapped. We speak more clearly than they, perhaps, or walk faster; we have the use of all our limbs, while they are without them. And they have a vision of life, of us, a vision of God, which is different. We thank God for our differences.

It has taken us a long, long time to recognise the richness of life; to accept from our friends the paintings done with the mouth, the wisdom offered to us through waving hands and words spelled out on a spelling board. It is not so long ago that we believed that it was impossible for a person we called handicapped to be a genius. Now we have come to acccept such things. God would not have allowed us to be so different from each other unless there was some special wisdom, some immense gift, that would come to us through such suffering. When the God of love creates us so different from each other, it is not because he has made a mistake, or because his creation has gone wrong. When he looks on his whole creation, he still sees that it is good.

Saying that is not to say we have explained it all, or that we are content that we should learn wisdom through other people's pain. We acknowledge the infinity of God's creative power when we admit that there are many things in his creation which we shall never understand: 'What man indeed can know the intentions of God? Who can divine the will of the Lord? The reasonings of mortals are unsure and our intentions unstable; for a perishable body weighs down the soul. . . it is hard enough for us to work out what is on earth, laborious to know what lies within our reach, who then can discover what is in the heavens?'

When our Lord was on earth he met many people who suffered appallingly; we do not understand why he did not cure them all. He met many people who were different; we do not understand why he allowed so many differences to cut us off from each other, unhearing, unspeaking, immovable. How does the suffering, the isolation of his people serve his purposes? We do not know. What we do know is that there is a blessed fellowship of suffering in which Christ the Lord is always present, a fellowship which to a greater or lesser degree we are all called upon to join. We join that Christ-fellowship of suffering with more or less grace, with more or less kindness and wisdom, in the measure we have understood those who have joined it before us, and those who have lived in it all their lives.

When one of our friends who has known so much suffering is now for the first time in life face to face with God, without pain, we must be joyful. And we are profoundly thankful too. If we have shared the wisdom of people whom God has made so different, we have seen a vision of God which no one else of our friends could have given us.

Though this outer man of ours may be falling into decay, the inner man is renewed day by day. Yes, the troubles which are soon over, though they weigh little, train us for the carrying of a weight of eternal glory which is out of all proportion to them. And so we have no eyes for things that are visible, but only for things that are invisible; for visible things last only for a time, and the invisible things are eternal. (2 Cor 4: 16-18).

*Des Wilson*

# Bread – Taken, Blessed, Broken, Given

*Reading:* Mk 14:22-25

For years her family have known that Margaret would not live to see a full adult life. For years they have been aware that this day would come sooner rather than later. And for years they and many friends of the family have learned to treasure the very special presence of Margaret with us. But perhaps only now – in spite of all that advance knowledge – only now do we begin to realise how much we have lost and how blessed we were to have been with her at all.

We remember that at his Last Supper, Jesus gave us himself in four special gestures: he took the bread, blessed it, broke it, and gave it to his friends. And does that not find an echo in the short life-story of Margaret? In reverse order perhaps. God gave Margaret to us, and a real gift she was. She was broken in a sense, unable to enter into many of the usual things of childhood and youth. But she was blessed with a unique ability to awaken our hearts, to draw us together around her, so that her blessing became our blessing and our humanity blossomed in her presence. She was indeed given, broken, blessed, and now she is taken back by God. They will enjoy one another.

And what of us who are filled today with sadness for ourselves and yet a strange wordless happiness for Margaret? Perhaps we could learn through her something utterly simple about God's shaping of our life stories. Like the bread at this Eucharist, we too are *taken* by God, each life chosen for a particular and unique purpose. Like the bread and like Margaret, each of us is *blessed* in different ways, with talents, friends, grace, and hunger to live with love. Like the bread each of us is *broken* somewhere in life – where we run into failure or darkness or some shadow. And yet we are being broken from our selfishness that we, like the bread, might be *given* more and so make this world a bit more like the Kingdom.

Today we both mourn and rejoice. Perhaps it is not really for ourselves that we should mourn but for those who never in life have had the chance of knowing a Margaret. And perhaps it is not only for Margaret that we rejoice. We rejoice that through her we can glimpse something of the simple pattern of God's plan for each of us – the story of the bread, taken, blessed, broken, and given. It is the story of Jesus rewritten in every life but clearer in some than in others. This morning we pray in thanksgiving for Margaret in whose short life that divine story was so beautifully visible for all to see.

*Michael Paul Gallagher SJ*

# Sign of Contradiction

*Reading:* Lk 2:25-35

Somewhere in the flat stones before the temple Simeon saw Joseph and the mother full of pride in this, her first born son. She knew the child was special for Gabriel had said so in the quietness of a spring day in Galilee, but Simeon had seen pain in the promise and a sword of suffering across the heart now brimming with joy. This child, he told her, would be a sign of contradiction.

This morning the words of an old man of biblical times ring out across the pain, prayer and parting of this day. This person, whom we honour by the presence of so many friends today, was indeed a sign of contradiction.

In a world of divison, he held out the open arms of acceptance.

In a world of borders, he saw no lines of divison.

In a world of mistrust, he called everyone a friend.

In a world of transgression, he treasured everyone as a fellow pilgrim.

In a world of ambition, he measured us all by the heart and not the head.

In a world of prudence, he was indeed a man of contradiction.

Weeks from now we will raise a headstone to this child of God. We will search for words to describe his living among us and we will never find the just expression of his presence because you and I will still go on measuring ourselves against each other and will seek security behind our man-made borders. We will measure out our forgiveness in petty gestures and will ration our love to those we think deserve it.

Thank God this child of his is well beyond our little limits and limitations. We thank God for the challenge he offered you and me, the challenge of looking into our lives and asking ourselves where is the joy lost in living, the wisdom lost in learning and the love lost in loving only ourselves. This child of God is wrapped up in his eternity while we, with scaled eyes, didn't see the gentle challenge of Jesus Christ behind the soft, sad eyes of the one, who for the past few years, had dwelt amongst us.

*John J McCullagh*

# God's Loudspeaker

*Readings:* Phil 3:20-21. Mt 19:13-15

The Church's liturgy for the funeral of a child may show little grief: the priest wears white vestments, the little coffin is white, and the readings and prayers echo a joyous note which may seem out of keeping with the sorrow of the mourners. But the Church, while in no way denying the real grief of parents and family, wishes to assure them that their child, who was adopted by God through baptism, already enjoys eternal happiness in heaven. The Mass and the prayers are offered for the consolation of the parents. What a consolation for any parent to know with all the assurance of their faith that a child of theirs, a living synthesis of both of them, is now among the saints in heaven!

In the case of a handicapped child there are added consolations. The parents of a handicapped child have known a mysterious mixture of joy and sorrow through their child. As this young couple sit here today in the front seat, they will no doubt recall the happiness of their wedding day when they were on kneelers even nearer to the altar than they are today. As they pledged their love for life in the presence of Christ, his priest and the community, they were solemnly asked: 'Are you willing to accept the children God may send you and bring them up in accordance with the laws of Christ and his Church?' 'We are,' they replied. In due course there was the joy that they were to include, into the circle of their love, a child. But in the midst of joy came the traumatic announcement that their child was handicapped, an imperfect copy of their joint persons. For a time they were shattered. But, gradually, as they recovered from the shock, they took this little one to their hearts, giving it even more love and attention then they would have given the normal child.

This is no easy programme for a young couple. Caring for any child is not easy, but caring for a handicapped child can involve enormous sacrifices, sleepless nights, problems with relatives and neighbours who do not know whether to congratulate or sympathise with the young parents and, consequently, make an awkward attempt at doing one or other, or else avoid both. But the young couple coped and found inner strength they never realised they possessed – strength they would never have known they had were it not for this experience.

They must have often wondered why all children are not born perfect physically and mentally. They must have wondered why any innocent child should suffer as their child. Above all today they must

71

wonder why, when they had adjusted to the situation and had become so deeply attached to this child, it is suddenly taken from them. These are normal questions for people in their situation, and they are abnormally difficult to answer. The answer must lie in the suffering of Christ who, though innocent, endured death on a cross to redeem and save us. In so doing, he joined love to suffering and gave to something, in itself negative, an immense potential for good in the world. The sufferer plays an active part in saving the world with Christ. Viewed from this standpoint, suffering has a wonderful value both for the sufferer and for all mankind.

In particular, the handicapped have a misson in the modern world of which we are only gradually becoming aware. First, they recall modern man to the value of simplicity, affection and complete trust. They remind us that there are more precious things than material goods, power and influence. Their very helplessness is God's loudspeaker to a world numbed with mass communications. The handicapped call forth generosity and love from parents, brothers and sisters, and neighbours which would otherwise remain untapped. If there was no wounded man by the wayside, there would never have been a Good Samaritan!

But most important of all. Those who share Christ's suffering and death – and this baptised handicapped child, who has just died, shares both in a very special way – already have a share in his glorious resurrection. As St Paul assures us: 'Christ will transfigure our bodies into copies of his own glorious body.' Perfect copies this time we can be sure. But we must not forget that Christ's risen body still bore the marks of his passion. A reminder surely that the unsightly wounds of this world became the marks of glory in the next.

*Dermot Clifford*

# The Least of His Brothers

*Readings:* Mt 25:31-40

Today this restless little life is stilled. The wounded nervous system and awkward limbs have come to rest and the incoherent words of life have, at last, found their meaning. So much of life is predictable: the sun will rise and set, people will be born, flourish for a time, decay into old age and will go to God in death. Now and again, the ebb and flow of life is interrupted when, in the life of one man, we are forced to lift our eyes from the earth and question our purpose and the progress of mankind. What does Christ say to you and me today in the discord of this life that is joined to his in resurrection?

For us, I think, who ration our forgiveness and pencil in our family pride, Christ asks that we look even closer at this sign of contradiction and the lessons scribbled on the seeming uselessness of this life. For here we saw the acceptance of all men who differ in colour, creed or Christianity. Here we saw forgiveness in the face of callousness and cruelty. Here we saw gratitude for the gift of time and patience from parents. Here we saw joy when one small achievement compensated for hours of frustration and repeated failures.

Perhaps we are the restless ones. We wound each others' nervous systems. We mutter incoherent words of love, forgiveness or sympathy. You and I gathered here are indeed the handicapped. The dead child was the still point in the storm of life in this troubled century. The one who was called handicapped was free and full of God.

Today Jesus calls this creation to himself and this community is the poorer for his passing as we bow our heads to the problems of our days. Jesus Christ, handicapped himself, because eternity was wrapped up in a child of time on a Christmas night in Bethlehem, has welcomed one of the least of his brothers home.

Meanwhile, we will go back to measuring ourselves against each other and reckoning our remaining days in the calendar of ordinary man.

*John J McCullagh*

73

# Refined in the Furnace

*Readings:* Qo 3:1-8. Rom 8:18-25. Mt 13:31-35

In his message to the sick and handicapped at Knock, the Pope said that 'pain and sorrow are never endured alone or in vain. . . The death of Jesus on the cross has given human suffering a new value and a new dimension.' He assured his listeners that they were collaborating with Jesus *in the salvation of the world.* The Pope insisted that all human pain has a divine meaning, and can be offered up for a divine purpose. 'By your suffering you help Jesus in his work of salvation,' he told the sick.

John did not enjoy good health for most of his life. After his accident he was severely handicapped and could not get about as other men. He suffered very great physical pain as well as mental anguish and for many years was confined to the house. Yet he never complained. His patient endurance had a purifying effect. He had become a strong, silent man, whom God had refined in the furnace of suffering.

A handicapped person is called to exercise in a very real sense the virtues of faith, hope and charity. He must have faith *in himself,* to overcome his disabilities, or at least to be reconciled to his situation. He must have faith *in others,* because he needs their help and depends so much on them for most things. He must have faith *in God,* whose providence in some strange and incomprehensible way, has allowed him to be struck down. This triple exercise of faith is almost heroic. He seemed to realise how important it was for him to keep on trusting in himself, in his family and friends and not least, in God. In the same way, he was called on to practise hope and charity, and it was in doing this that he developed a nobleness of character and strength of spirit.

We must have equal faith and believe that God has the power to give back our life on the last day. On that day, all those who have passed through this life handicapped or in some way unable to live as other men, will be changed and given back a complete and perfect body. St Paul assures us of this when he writes to the Corinthians:

> We shall all be changed. This will be instantaneous, in the twinkling of an eye, when the last trumpet sounds. It will sound, and the dead will be raised, imperishable.

And surely our consolation must be complete when we reflect on the final words of St Paul on the subject of death: 'Death is swallowed up in victory.' For John death has become a victory.

*Mark Tierney OSB*

# A Terrible Beauty

*Reading:* Mt 25:31-40

Mothers never forget birthdays. They have good reason to remember. No birth is easy. The birth of a handicapped child cuts deep into a mother's memory. Thomas was no exception. When it was tactfully revealed that he was severely deformed, mother went numb with shock and horror. 'It wasn't hers,' she kept repeating. 'Somebody has made a terrible mistake.' But there was no mistake. It was hers all right. When she left hospital a week later, Thomas came with her. They have literally been inseparable ever since. That was twelve years ago. Now Thomas is dead and well-meaning friends say: 'It must be a great relief to her.' But relief is not what she feels at all. She feels a huge, gaping emptiness in her life.

Thomas had given them so much. His utter helplessness, his absolute need of her, brought out reserves of strength she never even thought she possessed. Before she had Thomas, she was a self-centred, slightly-spoilt, pleasure-loving girl. Thomas' twisted little body was the sunshine that made her blossom as a person and a mother. And look at father. He was a gay, devil-may-care, good-time Charlie when she first met him. People said they were well-matched. Two of a kind. Now he is a home-loving, family man, deeply concerned about her and the children. There is a gentleness, sensitiveness about their oldest boy, quite untypical of his age. And the girls are a lot less selfish, a lot less spoilt. Thomas had brought out the best in all of them. His uncomplaining presence unconsciously set the tone. In the words of the poem, they were:

> All changed, changed utterly;
> A terrible beauty is born.

Christianity has always regarded the misfit and the outcast not as a blot on humanity, much less the faulty product of a nodding Creator, but as a treasure. It is no coincidence that the central parables are those like the Lost Sheep, the Prodigal Son, etc. Nor is it surprising that it should be in 'the least of the brethren' that Christ chose to reveal himself. Their contribution is of the highest order because they contribute to the more elusive quality of life itself. Without these crippled little witnesses, we would soon degenerate into ungrateful and uncaring automatons. The maimed, so often man's rejects, are in fact God's own gentry.

*Liam Swords*

75

# Take Up Your Cross

*Reading:* Mk 8:34

In his book *No Man is an Island* (page 122), Thomas Merton made the thought-provoking comment that we do not live more fully merely by doing more, seeing more, tasting more, experiencing more. What some of us need to discover is that we will not begin to live more fully until we have the courage to do and see and taste and experience much less.

So easily we divide the world into handicapped and people like ourselves. Is it fear which is at the root of such a tendency? In recent years, thank God, there has been a welcome discovery of the value of the handicapped people in our society, of their inestimable value as people, of their real contribution to our community and perhaps of the distinctive message which they have for all of us. Handicapped people show us that we cannot judge people by their material contribution to society. A brief reflection on history shows us how much people who were handicapped in one way or another have written their names across the pages of history. Augustus, the greatest of the Roman Emperors, had a stomach ulcer. Julius Ceasar, one of the greatest generals, was an epileptic. Admiral Nelson was violently sea-sick every time he put to sea. Ignatius had his kidney problem. Libermann his epilepsy. The list is endless. I think especially of St Paul who had his *thorn in the flesh* (epilepsy? malaria?). Not surprisingly he begged the Lord to take it away from him but he received the answer: 'My grace is sufficient for you, for in weakness power reaches perfection' (2 Cor 12:9).

'In the evening of life,' said St Augustine, 'we are judged on love.' We do not choose our talents, our handicaps, our temperaments. But rather each person is chosen in God's love to show aspects of his love to the world, to grow and to help others grow towards the perfection of love. Paul saw the whole universe and not just people as imperfect, as groaning towards a fulfilment of love which will give meaning to everything which we now suffer. A handicap is a reminder that no person is an island, that people need each other, need opportunities to serve others. We help one another even by giving people opportunities to serve us, to show love to us. As the blind poet Milton realised, we also can serve God who only stand and wait.

*Sean P Kealy CSSp*

# Requiem of a Prophet

*Reading:* 1 Kings 19:11-13

Would it surprise you if I said that we come here today for the requiem of a prophet? When the word 'prophet' comes to mind, we think of those single-named preachers who wandered the hill country of Judea and the streets of old Jerusalem shouting God's word to a people who didn't want to hear too much of it. Many of them, you remember, got no hearing. Many, indeed, were laughed at and Jerusalem, the 'killer of the prophets', spilled their blood too often onto its dusty streets.

The age of the prophet has not yet passed. There are men and women upon whom the Spirit, promised by God, has been given. These are the people who turn the sacred values of our world upside down. There are still old men who dream dreams of peace, freedom from hunger and love across the face of the earth. And there are young men and women who have a vision that will make the dream, one day, a reality. But not all prophesying is thundering God's word or threatening his wrath. God still speaks to us in silence. If we look this morning at the life of the one who has been taken from us we will see this dead, gentle prophet as one who experienced what Elijah, one of the old prophets, learned on a mountain a long time ago.

'Go out and stand on the mountain before the Lord,' he was told:
Then the Lord himself came by. There came a mighty wind, so strong it tore the mountains and shattered the rock before the Lord, but the Lord was not in the wind. After the wind came an earthquake. But the Lord was not in the earthquake. After the earthquake came a fire. But the Lord was not in the fire. And after the fire came the sound of a gentle breeze. (1 Kings 19:11-13)

This human being, called and marked by God for a special mission in life, spoke to us, even in the quietness of his living. Perhaps we never listened. We live in an age when man's worth is largely measured by his possessions. Even the joy we have seems to be bought on credit. But this child of God asked us where is the knowledge we lost in information, and where is the wisdom for all our knowledge? In a world where we are refugees running from one crisis to the next, he challenged our anxiety with his peace of mind and sense of security, which he found in the goodness of those who cared for him.

God did give him a restricted life. Maybe he is asking the rest of us, whose handicaps are not so obvious, to begin to realise that man is not measured totally in the eyes of the Almighty by intelligence tests, academic brains, feats of endurance, or outstanding skills. This child of God took life one day at a time, people, one at a time, friendship, one embrace at a time. He never spoke about love, he lived it.

As we go home from his final resting place perhaps we will grasp one precious moment of silence and ask why God sent this challenge to us and see if, in that life, there was a lesson for all of us who carry the smallest set-back as a calamitous cross.

*John J McCullagh*

---

*Suggested Alternative Scripture Readings:*

Psalms 9:1-2, 9-10. 10:14, 17-18. 70:1, 4-5. 72:1-4, 12-14, 18-20. 107:1-3, 10-16, 19-22, 39-43. 118:1-9, 17-24, 28, 29. 119:169-176. 146:1-10. 147:1-7.
Ecclesiasticus 33:7-14.

Matthew 5:1-12.
Lk 23:23-33, 39-43, 44-49, 24:1-6.
John 11:21-27.

# 7
## Death of the Elderly

## *Born Again*

*Reading :* John 3:1-8

Few events of world significance could have been less spectacular than the first Easter morning. The sight that greeted those two early morning joggers, Peter and John, was not the risen Lord, nor even his crucified remains as they had hoped to find, but an empty tomb. 'What have they done with him?' Mary Magdalen asked the first one she met. Mary who knew and grieved for the human Christ so deeply, could not see, beyond grief and the grave, the risen Christ. An empty tomb. No more. The astonishing truth came later. Christ was the first born from the dead. He had broken the death-barrier.

The empty tomb explained everything. An empty womb after a new birth. Life is changed, not ended. Birth and death have much in common. The child in a mother's womb has a cosy existence. All its needs are provided for. All its wants are taken care of. Nothing can harm it. Nothing can hurt it. Its life-support system is all but foolproof. But life is more than food and warmth and security. If the child is to grow to its full potential, it must leave the mother's womb. It must quit one world for another. It must die to be born. And birth like death is never easy. Most people enter the world crying. Few leave it without regret. The unknown holds terror for everyone.

And yet if the child in the womb could only have reflected on itself and its birth, there was nothing really to fear. It was well-equipped for another world. Had it not two little feet that could walk? Soon there would be great parental pride and excitement when it took its first faltering steps. And there would be other important steps to take on the road through life. It had hands, too, hands that would shake more than a baby's rattle, hands that would reach out to greater things. Eyes, now tightly shut, that soon would open up to mother's smile, sun-rise, a Renoir, flowers, light and darkness. Ears that could hear no more than the deafening drum-beat of a mother's heart, would hear bird-song and Beethoven, laughter and loves' sweet nothings and the word of God. Ephetha! A tongue that would speak, communicate and sing the marvels of creation. Its own little heart would take over life supporting and loving. But first it must die. It must be expelled from its mother's womb.

The world is a womb. Mother earth. The time comes when we have gone full term. Three score and ten is as normal for second delivery as nine months was for our first. It can be premature or overdue. Some babies cling to the womb longer. Some cling to life longer. Womb-bound they are reluctant to part. Parents, in turn, become dependant on life-support systems. Second childhood! Delivery is difficult for some, easy for others, inevitable for all. The cycle is irreversible. 'Unless a man be born again,' Christ told a puzzled Nicodemus, 'he cannot enter the kingdom of heaven.' There is nothing to fear, nothing to regret. When we shake off this mortal coil we will begin a new life, eternal life. We have vast untapped talents that can only blossom there.

> Eye hath not seen, nor ear heard,
> nor hath it entered into the heart of man
> to conceive what God hath in store
> for those whom he loves.

*Liam Swords*

# In the Fullness of Time

'In the fullness of time', that phrase from Scripture comes to mind as we pray for the deceased. His was a long and full life, the biblical four score and more. Even as we gather with sadness, that sadness is shot through with a deep serenity and a great gratitude for his life. And when we say before God that we are thankful to have known and loved someone like the deceased, we are in fact thanking God for revealing something of himself yet again in human form.

It was only in Jesus Christ that we saw the glory and goodness of God fully shining in a human face. And yet it is also true that in the goodness of every human being, there is another if different revelation of God, incomplete, flawed, but nevertheless a mirror of his love.

Why, as I said, is our mourning mingled with such quiet gratitude today? Because we have been in the presence of someone who helped us to glimpse God. Borrowing in a word from another religion, would it be too much to say that everyone is called to be a 'reincarnation' of God? Did not St Paul say: 'not I that live but Christ that lives in me'?

We are here in this life to echo the life of Christ, to grow in wisdom and age like him, to reach out like him in healing to the wounded of the world, to love children, to have compassion on the weak and suffering, to make our hearts known to our friends, to take up our crosses, to forgive others and be forgiven, to find mountain places for prayer, to have the courage to oppose evil. . . That litany could continue but these facets of Christ himself are alive for us today because we glimpsed them in the struggling life and love of the deceased. Struggling because, like all of us, he was imperfect; yet a struggling love because through a long life he learned from God to let go of himself and to live for others. And now he has let go finally.

Our consolation today comes from gratitude for him, for God in him, for Christ glimpsed through him. But our real consolation comes in 'the faith that looks through death' (Wordsworth), in the hope that gathers us here, the hope that as the deceased shared in Christ's way of life, and now shares his death, so he will also belong with Christ in his new life. We cannot understand that hope and yet we can have it. We cannot always explain that faith and yet it makes sense to our hearts today. We cannot put words on that love of God and yet when we have seen it in a good person's life and death, we too are able to recognise it, and to say a deeper and more grateful 'yes' to God.

*Michael Paul Gallagher SJ*

# Deep Roots

*Readings:* Job 12:10-14. 2 Tim 2:8-13. Jn 12:23-28

No two people are alike and it is this very uniqueness which makes us loved not only by our fellow men, but especially by God. That wonderful phrase of our Lord in the Gospel about 'the hairs of our head being numbered by our heavenly Father', and that 'not even one sparrow can fall to the ground without God knowing about it', is surely proof of the value which God puts on every human life. We are here for a purpose, a divine purpose, and the hand of God has been laid on us all. The hand of God was laid on the deceased and never more than during his last days. The dignity with which we face death is very much the fruit, if not the proof, of the dignity and uprightness shown throughout life.

The lesson of old age is that of endurance and faith. In all our lives there are the valleys and the hills, the good times and the bad times, the successes and the failures, the joys and the sorrows. We have a very short span of life given us by God, and those who live the longest become deeply aware that this time is not given so much for our enjoyment, but rather to work out our salvation. None of us is ever given sufficient time to sink our roots too deeply into this world. With advancing age, we learn that we have not here a lasting kingdom, but wait for one which is to come.

No one can work out his salvation alone. We need examples all around us, to point out a better way, a surer road, a safer path. The deceased was a wonderful exemplar of old world values. In our space age, and atomic age, many of us are lost or at least confused. Science seems to have turned not only our physical world, but also our spiritual world upside down. The solid rock of common sense, as well as the practice of Christian gentlemanly virtues, must not be lost sight of in our modern world. Honesty, integrity and goodness, are not met with so often today and more's the pity. The deceased lived as a gentleman and died like a gentleman, concerned right up to the end lest he cause any inconvenience or trouble to anyone. Above all, he showed his great appreciation of the services and devoted attention of those good people who attended him day and night during his final illness. Our prayer this morning is that he now enjoys that peace and happiness for which he pined throughout his long life, and that God has now taken him into his safe keeping.

*Mark Tierney OSB*

# The Bread of Eternal Life

*Readings:* Is 25:6-9. Jn 6:51-58

In offering this funeral Mass, we are offering the greatest of all prayers – the Eucharist. We are united with the prayer of Christ in his offering of himself to the Father for us. More than that, we are proclaiming why it is that, even in the face of death and the sadness of our parting, we have hope. We believe that God will 'swallow up death for ever'. He has already begun to do so in the resurrection of Jesus, who 'being raised from the dead will never die again; death no longer has any dominion over him' (Rom 6:9). We know that he is beyond death and that he has invited us to follow him through death into new life.

That invitation and promise are expressed in the Eucharist when the risen Jesus gives himself to us: 'If anyone eats of this bread, he will live for ever' (Jn 6:50). The deceased ate the bread of life many times during his (her) long life; many times the Lord came to him (her) in Communion to remind him (her) that he will come again and take us to himself so that where he is we may be also (cf. Jn 14:3).

Death parts us from those we love, yet we are still one. We are gathered now in the presence of the same Christ around whom they are gathered . They are with Christ in a unity which we too hope to share fully when the promises of God are fulfilled for us. We are already beginning to share that eternal unity with him in the Eucharist. In the Mass, we proclaim our hope and our unity with all God's people, living and dead. What we are doing here, in spite of our sorrows and weaknesses and uncertainties, is what all those who have died in Christ are now doing in endless light, happiness and peace. By our Mass today, we express our unity with the deceased and pray that s(he) is in the presence of God for ever.

The risen Christ gives himself to us as the living bread come down from heaven. That bread of life is an anticipation of the feast which the Lord is making ready for all peoples. In that feast of eternal joy, every tear will be wiped away. The sadness will be over. We will clearly see the Lord who is with us now as an unseen presence. Together with our relatives and friends, living and dead, we will experience the full reality of his presence. Then, as Isaiah prophesied, we will be able to say:

This is the Lord; we have waited for him. . .
Let us be glad and rejoice in his salvation.

*+Donal Murray*

# Pile of Sand

*Reading:* Jn 15:13

Death never seems to come on time. For some, it comes too early, and for others, it comes too late. Just as a very tired child may still protest about having to go to bed, even though sleep is about to catch up with him, so it can be with the elderly. Just as the tired child has a right to sleep, so the elderly have a right to die. Death can be as natural as sleep.

For the Christian, it is the *living* that is the dying. Life itself is a whole series of deaths, dying to my pride, my possessions, my opinions, my comforts, for the sake of others. This dying is the greatest love of all, Jesus tells us (Jn 15:13). Death is like a pile of sand at the end of my life, which I am asked to take and sprinkle throughout my days, a little bit every day. In doing this I can come to the end of my life, and just fall quietly asleep; my dying will have taken place already. If I wait till the end of my life to die, it will be too late. The advantage of having a long life is that there has been time in which to do that dying.

Life is a journey from one birth to yet another birth, from the womb-life into the womb of life, into the fullness of life. There is a beautiful parallel between the beginning of life, with the infant and the end of life, with the elderly. There is a dependency, a nursing, a great need for others there that the intervening years may shroud. In more than name, it can, indeed, be a second childhood.

Bereavement is like an amputation. It takes some time for a person to adjust to having just one leg. It is the same with the loss that is bereavement. Grief is the price we pay for love. Grief and sorrow are as much part of life as joy and laughter. The tears of Jesus at the tomb of Lazarus were tears of love, not tears of despair. He told Martha that her brother would rise again (Jn 11:23). Even a bereavement that has long been expected and anticipated is never easy. Just as the mother surrenders her baby to the womb of life, and then has to deal with the pain of separation, the post-natal depression, so it is with the second birth we call death.

And so despite the pain of loss, we thank God for the life of the deceased and for the blessings that that life brought to so many. It is our Christian belief that we do not bury him now; he is with the Lord now, and we just bury the clothes, the outer garment, as it were, with the certain confidence that he will come back for them one day. Sleep well and peacefully. We don't begrudge you your rest.

*Jack McArdle SS CC*

# The Complete Life

*Reading:* Proverbs 31:10-31

There is, we know, a time for mourning and a time for joy. Today these two emotions will surely find a place together in our hearts. At the end of this long life it may be that the need to praise God is uppermost in our minds, because it is so clear how rich God's blessings have been. We can cheerfully cry out with the psalmist, 'My soul give thanks to the Lord and never forget all his blessings!' And at the same time, of course, we mourn for our hearts are heavy with sadness.

We have lost an old friend who was a mother to countless people – far more than just her own family – and a sister to all the world. She was one of those people with a huge heart who had room for everyone. So of course we are sad. Even though her dying was expected, there is a sense of loss, a feeling that there is unfinished business yet to be completed.

But, thankfully, woven into this there is deep gratitude to God for all this woman has been to us. We are happy because we know deep down that her life was complete, and that she was ready for God. We received much from her, and now we have had to let her go. An early Christian teacher once said: 'The glory of God is someone made fully alive.' She was an intensely alive person, wonderfully whole, and certainly her life gave glory to God.

She lived her life according to the Sermon on the Mount. She always had her sights raised to the horizon; she lived according to a great vision that was always beyond her reach but for which she was always striving. She saw the Commandments not as minimal rules to make sure of keeping on the straight and narrow, but as signposts to an ever more exciting life. She never gave up; she never said, 'I've done enough.' She knew she was blessed and rejoiced in that; she trusted absolutely in God; she prayed; she treated everyone who came to her with dignity and respect. She was a true disciple of the Lord.

She lived also as a member of the Church. She treasured her life in the Church and was closely and intimately part of everything that went on in the Church. She suffered when the Church suffered, and was deeply glad when the Church rejoiced. She gave herself generously to the Church, and happily received whatever the Church offered her. The sacraments were treasures for her daily living; they were the guarantees she looked for of the presence of God in her life, never more so than when she couldn't pay, or when times were bad.

And she lived too by the needs of others. She was one of those marvellous people who read other people's needs without in any way being patronising or offensive. She was the good samaritan, but the wounded person was scarcely conscious of her help. She bound up hearts that were broken, breathed gently on the smouldering flax, treated the crushed reed with great tenderness – and all in the most matter-of-fact and unfussy way.

At heart she was a simple person and like all simple people was open to everyone, particularly to the power of God. She was close to God, one of his dear friends. She had heard her calling from God and was obedient to it. Perhaps this was the secret of her life: like Mary she possessed an utterly faithful obedience. Like Mary she must have said: 'Be it done to me according to your word.'

And now she has stretched out her tired old hands for the last time and God has taken her to himself. Let us pray with hope and gratitude for the eternal rest of this valiant woman, and join again with the psalmist in his prayer: 'My soul give thanks to the Lord, and never forget all his blessings!'

*+David Konstant*

# Enduring Value

When a person dies after a long life, I suppose there is some easing of the sorrow of bereavement. N. lived her good span of years and has now gone back to God. She was called to suffer a very hard last six months or so, when her body and indeed her mind struggled with the pain of injuries inflicted as a result of a violent accident. Though advanced in years, her death is a separation and a sad loss for her family.

Through the liturgy of the Mass we gather in friendship here to ask God to take care of her now that her earthly life is over. Through this Mass we share in the mystery of Christ who has gone through death before us and has by his resurrection bequeathed to us all the one sure ground of hope and fulfilment. Death is a mystery with which we can hardly grapple at all satisfactorily without faith; death in itself leaves us puzzled and forlorn.

Those of us who have been raised since childhood in Christianity become perhaps over-accustomed to the truths of this faith. Over the years we develop an inadvertence to one remarkable belief of Christianity. It is a belief not found with the same emphasis and clarity in any other world religion or social ideology for that matter. The unique importance and value that the Christian faith attaches to the individual person; that he or she is known and loved for himself, for herself, by God from all eternity. This immensity and exclusivity of God's love for each one of us, no matter how imperfect we are, this is something beyond our natural ability to grasp. So strong is this belief in the intrinsic worth of the individual, so strong is this Christian conviction, that it carries over into a belief that somehow his or her value endures beyond this earthly life. Each person is so valuable in the sight of God that he or she is destined to enjoy a permanence which we call 'everlasting life'.

We can understand very little about this: very little, but enough for it to be the raw material for faith to work on. It is Jesus Christ who enlightens this basic, and often dim enough, appreciation of the absolute value of the individual person. Through the teaching of Christ, through his own life, death and resurrection, the modest but sure hope for the future is opened up to us. In this hope we pray for N. this morning, that she may enjoy eternal life.

*Tom Stack*

# I Come to do Your Will

It is never easy to accept death, but there are times when it comes as a blessing. At Mass this morning giving thanks for the life of Annie and praying for her we know that in many ways her death is a blessing.

She had a long life and for the last twenty years of her life she suffered so much. She suffered for a long time. So the sadness of her loss is tempered with the knowledge that now her suffering is over.

I shared with Annie, more than once, the little conversation that St Thérèse is supposed to have had with the Lord. In the midst of her own pain she was asking the Lord why she had so much pain, so much suffering. The Lord said to her that he always treated his friends that way. To this she retorted, 'Then it is not surprising you have so few friends.'

The one thing that was absolutely clear with Annie was that she was a friend of the Lord. She had an easy familiarity with him. It came through all she was asked to be and to do by the Lord.

I can never understand why the Lord asks so much of some people. But I do know that in response to suffering so many people, and Annie was one of them, grow as people. Physically she seemed to shrink. She seemed to get smaller as the pain and suffering took its toll. But no matter how she shrunk I always felt small in her presence. She was a woman of real depth. She was a real person and she brought God's love and God's truth into our world.

The number of people who were touched by her. They might have gone in to help her in her later years, yet they were the ones who were really helped. They were the ones who were given so much by knowing and meeting Annie. Now she has finished her journey. She has been asked for so much during her life that there was not much of her left to give.

But now that has gone. She is still giving us the benefit of her faith and her love and her true wisdom. Our lives are the richer for knowing her. Our lives have been blessed by her presence.

A little lady, in a little house, on a little road – yet God has done wonderful things through her.

*J. Harry Stratton*

# In the Shadow of God's Presence

*Readings:* Wis 3:1. Rom 8:39. 2 Cor 5:1

The great dividing line of our existence in this world is the gap between life and death. There is nothing extraordinary about dying and about death. It's one of the most natural things in the world. Once we accept life, we accept too that life will end, that someday, somewhere, sometime, someone will attend your funeral, someone will stand by my grave. Winter follows spring, decay follows growth, death is the final act of life.

And yet no matter how inevitable death may be, no matter how clearly we have it in our minds that all life will pass away, death always seems to take us by surprise. When the hand of death is laid on the shoulder of someone close and important to us death becomes not a natural and acceptable experience but a strange and sometimes frightening encounter with the unknown, a permanent and disquieting silence after an extended life-time of movement and activity.

The deceased belonged to a generation who like to have their preparations well made, whether for a short journey in this life or an even longer journey to God in the next. Her generation too seems to be more comfortable with death than we are. Not indeed that they took it for granted. But they had a feel for death and a respect for life that we are in danger of losing today. They had a sense of the all-pervading presence of God in good times and in bad. And they were able to relate the events and happenings of their lives to the presence of God among them in the most natural of ways. Maybe it was because their lives were lived continually in the shadow of God's presence. They had a sense that God was close to them, that God was calling them to a better and happier place when the struggles of life would be over:

> For we know that when the tent that we live in on earth is folded up, there is a house built by God for us, an everlasting home not made with human hands (2 Cor 5:1).

And for that reason they had about them a great sense of reverence, a dignity and a respect that came, not just from the wisdom of long years lived well, but from a sense of what was right and true and good, a sense that 'nothing could come between them and the love of God made visible in Christ Jesus' (Rom 8:39), a sense that 'the souls of the virtuous are in the hands of God. No torment shall ever touch them' (Wis 3:1). They had sharp sense of God's presence that flowed into the values around which they organised their lives, into the faith, hope and love that they planted in the soil of their children's lives, that they expressed through their extraordinary loyalty to their Sunday Mass and their devotion to family prayer.

The word 'saintliness' would embarrass them but a lesser word hardly describes a people so touched by the finger of God, a people who could incorporate pain and effort in the texture of their Christian lives, a people who saw their religion not as a burden or a nuisance but as a privileged way of life that gave richness and meaning to life lived on God's earth. God for them was in the bits and pieces of every day, in the silence and stillness of their lives, in the sense of awe and wonder that we have so easily dispelled in the prosperity and materialism of more recent years.

So today let us not so much mourn her death as celebrate her homecoming, with thanks to God for her long life, for the example her faith gives us, for the lessons that we learned from her about living well and dying well.

May her gentle soul rest contentedly today in the happiness of God's home.

*Brendan Hoban*

---

*Suggested Alternative Scripture Readings:*

Genesis 49:29-33.
Numbers 23:9-10.
Psalms 3:1-6. 4:1-2, 6-8. 20:1-5. 21:1-6. 25:1-15. 33:13-22. 34:3-22. 37:23-28, 37-40a. 40:1-2, 5-8, 13-14, 17. 51:1-15. 66:5, 10-12, 16-20. 68:3-6, 9-10, 19-20. 71:1-8, 18-22. 77:1-14. 90:1-12. 91:1-6, 14-16. 100. 102:23a-27. 103:1-18. 119:25-32. 121:1-8. 138:1-3, 7-8. 139:7-18. 143:1-2, 5-10.
Ecclesiastes 3:1-8. 12:1-8.
Ecclesiasticus 11:14-17, 22-24, 26-30. 14:12-20. 18:8-14. 41:1-7. 44:1-15 *(illustrious men)*.
Wisdom 4:7-15.
Lamentations 3:17-26.

1 Corinthians 15:20-28.
2 Corinthians 5:1, 6-10.
Matthew 5:1-12. 25:31-46
Mark 15:33-39. 16:1-6